JUST THE BEST

List of Cooks

Julia Aitken
Carroll Allen
Julian Armstrong
Elizabeth Baird
Fran Berkoff
Pierre Berton
Beverley Burge
Kate Bush
Peter Cochrane
Julie Cohen
Pam Collacott
Judith Comfort
Gay Cook
Allison Cumming
Cynthia David
Rollande DesBois
Thelma Dickman
Dufflet
Eileen Dwillies
Charlotte Empringham
Nancy Enright
Carol Ferguson
Rita Feutl
Judith Finlayson
Margaret Fraser
Alison Fryer
Barb Holland
Patricia Jamieson
Marion Kane
Joanne Kates
Dinah Koo
Alice Krueger
Suzanne Leclerc
Anne Lindsay

Marilyn Linton
Leslie Lucas
Mary McGrath
Barbara McQuade
Catha McMaster
Jan Main
Rhonda May
Susan Mendelson
Umberto Menghi
Barbara Mercer
Rose Murray
Vicki Newbury
Marie Nightingale
Margo Oliver
Daphna Rabinovitch
Michelle Ramsay
Iris Raven
Rose Reisman
Noël Richardson
Monda Rosenberg
Rosie Schwartz
Judy Schultz
Kathleen Sloan
Kay Spicer
Edna Staebler
Bonnie Stern
Anita Stewart
Ladka Sweeney
Kathleen Walker
Julie V. Watson
Lucy Waverman
Kasey Wilson
Cynthia Wine

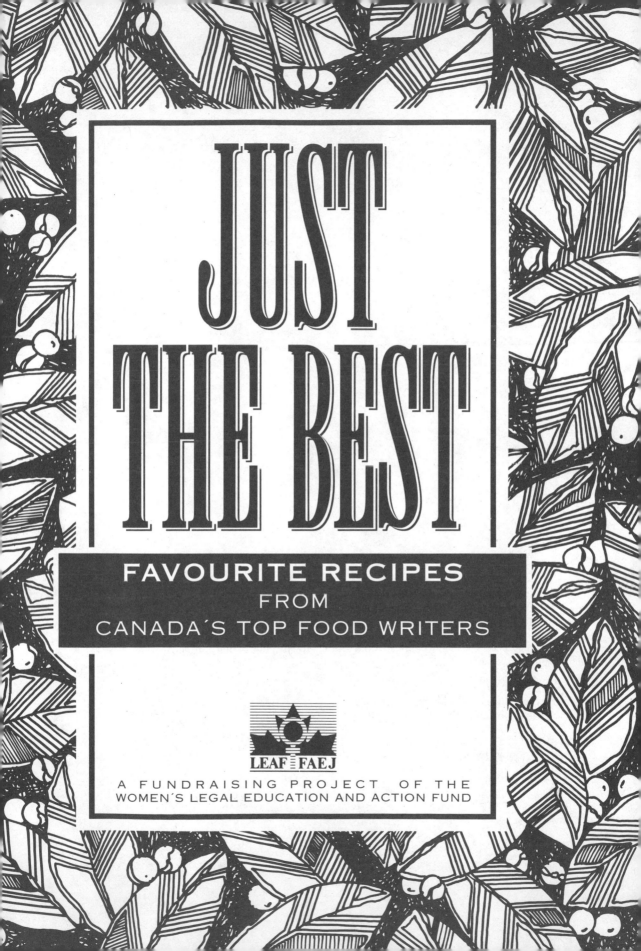

JUST THE BEST

FAVOURITE RECIPES
FROM
CANADA'S TOP FOOD WRITERS

LEAF ✦ FAEJ

A FUNDRAISING PROJECT OF THE
WOMEN'S LEGAL EDUCATION AND ACTION FUND

Distributed in Canada by Macmillan Canada
(A division of Canada Publishing Corporation)

LEAF/FAEJ 489 rue College St., Ste. 403,
Toronto, Ontario M6G 1A5

Printed and bound in Canada by **Best Gagné**
Art Direction, Design and Production: Dori Burchat
Illustrations: Betty Biesenthal
Linotronic Output: Creative Copy & Design

Printed on paper
containing over 50%
recycled paper including
10% post-consumer fibre.

CONTENTS

Acknowledgements...ix

Introduction to LEAF xi

Choosing Wines...xiii

Appetizers..1

Soups 19

Salads...35

Chicken..49

Fish and Seafood 63

Meat 73

Vegetables..93

Pasta 107

Rice, Grains and Legumes..125

Cakes and Squares..139

Cookies, Muffins and Biscuits...155

Pies, Puddings and Cobblers 167

More Desserts and Drinks 179

Menus...188

Index 190

Federation of Women Teachers' Associations of Ontario

FWTAO is the professional organization of the 40,000 female elementary teachers in the public schools of Ontario, working towards equality for all members of society through advocacy for women and children and through leadership in educational change.

FWTAO was formed in 1918 and has over the years been successful in lobbying for:

- the right of married women to retain their jobs
- the right of pregnant women to job security and paid maternity leave
- pay equity for women
- protection of the rights of abused women and children
- mandatory affirmative action programmes
- increased support for education at the elementary level
- child centred programming
- access to non-traditional careers
- mandatory sexual harassment policies in the work place
- employment equity for women and visible minorities
- increased public action to end violence against women and children

FWTAO has been instrumental in the formation of and support for other women's activist groups such as the National Action Committee on the Status of Women and the Women's Legal Education and Action Fund.

The funds raised from sale of this cookbook by our members will be donated to women's shelters across Ontario.

Uncle Ben's

Uncle Ben's is proud to sponsor the Women's Legal Education and Action Fund's (LEAF) cookbook, an impressive Canadian cookbook that will hopefully become a permanent fixture in kitchens across Canada. This all-Canadian cookbook has been a labour of love. Developed on a volunteer basis and contributed to most generously by Canada's food writers, *Just the Best* offers delicious and nutritious recipes for everything from soup to rice.

As the consumption of rice in Canada continues to rise, rice is no longer simply a side dish, but has moved to the centre of the plate as a base for many tasty entrees. And with nutrition experts now recommending that 55 to 60 percent of all calories should come from "starchy" foods, rice is the perfect choice for family meals. It is low in fat and cholesterol, sodium free and a good source of two important B vitamins, niacin and thiamine. Versatile and easy to prepare, rice is a popular nutritious base for appetizers, salads, even desserts.

Just the Best provides a delicious array of rice recipes, including healthy Nutty Brown Rice with lightly toasted pecans, appetizing Rice with Fresh Spring Vegetables and traditional Jamaican Rice and Peas. For special occasions, Whole Baked Fish and Rice, garnished with fresh dill, and low-fat Lemon Herb Rice or Quick Pilaf with Pine Nuts will make an impressive addition to culinary repertoires.

Select Food Products Limited

Select Food Products Limited management and staff are proud to be associated with LEAF and wish to extend their congratulations for the pioneering work in the area of women's equality and hope for continued success.

The Cookbook Committee

Julia Aitken, Food Editor, *Homemaker's* magazine

Dori Burchat, Creative Director, Loblaws

Judith Finlayson, writer, and Chair of LEAF's National Fund-Raising Committee

Heather Hamilton, homemaker

Anne Lindsay, cookbook author and contributor to *Canadian Living* magazine

Marilyn Linton, Lifestyle Editor, the *Toronto Sun*

Christine Mullen, Product Developer, Loblaws

Rose Reisman, cookbook author

Barbara Schon, freelance editor

Denise Schon, Vice President and Publisher, Macmillan Canada

Carmel Shaffer, Director of Publicity and Advertising, Macmillan Canada

Ladka Sweeney, Product Developer, A&P

Cynthia Wine, Restaurant Critic, *The Toronto Star*

Acknowledgements

As Chair of LEAF's National Fund-raising Committee and co-chair of the Cookbook Committee, I'd like to take this opportunity to thank all of the people who made this cookbook a reality. First and foremost are my co-chair, Denise Schon, and the cookbook committee, a group of very talented and hard-working women who volunteered their time and energy with a remarkable degree of commitment. In the early stages of the project, this dynamic group solicited recipes from top food-writers across the country. A sub-committee composed of the food professionals, (Julia Aitken, Anne Lindsay, Marilyn Linton, Christine Mullen, Rose Reisman, Ladka Sweeney and Cynthia Wine) selected the best of these submissions. Hard choices had to be made. The recipes had to be simple and easy to follow, but they also had to offer something unique. The ingredients also had to be easily available. When you read through the book, you'll see that most of the selections qualify as healthy eating — relatively low in fat and high in fibre. However, a few special occasion recipes were so tempting that the committee ignored these criteria in favour of a gastronomic experience.

Once the recipes were selected, Ladka Sweeney and Christine Mullen tested them all. Only the best made it through this stage of selection. Marilyn Linton then went to work, writing introductions to all the recipes as well as biographies of the contributors. Anne Lindsay and Cynthia Wine developed the menus. And Rose Reisman, whose specialty is simplifying complicated recipes, went through the manuscript and provided cooking tips.

Then the editorial team, under the direction of Barbara Schon, began to work. Edna Barker, Gail Copeland, Meg Taylor and Wendy Thomas edited the recipes. Heather Hamilton took charge of in-putting all the copy onto disk. Dori Burchat both designed and produced the artwork with the help of Rony Zibara, and Janice Brett looked after many print production details. Thanks to Betty Biesenthal for the cover illustration.

Special thanks to Sally Armstrong, who in the course of a casual conversation suggested that since Canada has so many exceptional food writers, the best the way to do a cookbook for a women's organization was to ask them for their favourite recipes. And to Tony Aspler who made suggestions for appropriate wines to accompany the recipes.

Carmel Shaffer and Jacqueline Foley were a great help with promotion and marketing, and Marina Heidman was a lifesaver, organizing special sales to LEAF branches across the country.

Ron Besse and Bob Dees gave much encouragement and support throughout the process.

Uncle Ben's deserve special thanks for their early commitment to the project. As usual, the Federation of Women's Teachers of Ontario made a committment far above and beyond the call of duty. Thanks also to Select Foods for supporting this project.

To the LEAF staff and, of course, the many cooks who contributed their recipes, our thanks to all of you.

Judith Finlayson,
Chair, National Fund-raising Committee
The Women's Legal Education and Action Fund

Introduction to LEAF

Just The Best: Favourite Recipes From Canada's Top Food Writers is a fund-raising project of the Women's Legal Education and Action Fund (LEAF), a national, non-profit, voluntary organization which promotes equality for women through legal action and public education.

LEAF's roots extend from the massive mobilization of Canadian women that was organized around our new constitution in 1981. When it became clear that women's equality was not part of the constitutional debate, thousands of Canadian women fought to ensure that strong equality guarantees would be included. As a result of their efforts, Canada now has some of the strongest constitutional protections for women in the western world.

LEAF was established on April 17, 1985, the day the equality provisions came into force, by some of the women who had fought to have those provisions included in the Charter of Rights and Freedoms. They knew that strong words would mean little for women if the provisions were not tested in the courts.

Because charter litigation is extremely expensive, ordinary Canadians have little hope of undertaking a test case on their own. LEAF helps women with precedent setting cases to get their day in court. When LEAF takes on a case, it undertakes the necessary research, finds legal counsel for the case and pays all the expenses involved.

LEAF's successful track record and participation in a number of landmark cases has established its credibility in the courts. As a result it has earned the confidence of its constituency. Groups concerned with equal rights now regularly turn to LEAF for advice and expertise.

Since its inception, LEAF has won some major victories for Canadian women and families. Successes have been achieved in areas such as:

Sexual harassment: LEAF intervened in the cases of Diane Janzen and Tracey Govereau, two Winnipeg waitresses who were sexually harassed by an employee at work. The landmark decision recognized that sexual harassment is illegal because it is sex discrimination.

Pregnancy discrimination: LEAF intervened in the case of Brooks, Allen, and Dixon, three employees at Canada Safeway in Winnipeg who were denied company health benefits when they were pregnant. LEAF helped to win a Supreme Court ruling that pregnancy discrimination is illegal because it is sex discrimination.

Pay equity: LEAF supported the Equal Pay Coalition in its successful submission to the court that pay equity legislation must be interpreted to benefit the most disadvantaged workers, who are often women in female-dominated occupations. Nurses, who traditionally have been excluded from the act, won an important ruling that makes it possible for them, for pay equity purposes, to compare their wages to those of police employed by the same municipality.

Pornography: LEAF intervened to ensure that the obscenity provisions of the Criminal Code were upheld when they were challenged by owners of a video store in Manitoba. The Supreme Court recognized the connection between pornography and violence against women, as well as other aspects of women's inequality.

Security for rape survivors: LEAF as part of a coalition of seven community and women's organizations presented equality arguments at the Supreme Court when the Canadian Newspapers Company challenged Criminal Code provisions giving women who have been raped the right to choose whether or not their identity can be revealed in print and broadcast reports. The Supreme Court upheld this right.

These victories represent just a small sampling of LEAF's cases. In fact, LEAF has taken on more than 100 cases that challenge laws and government policies that discriminate against women. When Canada's so-called "rape shield" legislation was overturned in the fall of 1991, LEAF worked in consultation with women's groups from across the country as well as with the Minister of Justice to develop new legislation that would more effectively protect women and children who have been raped. LEAF currently has a full roster of cases on issues such as pensions, domestic violence and sexual assault.

Even though LEAF's lawyers donate their time — LEAF receives more than half a million dollars a year in donated legal time — the costs of cases are very high. When LEAF takes on a case, it must be prepared to argue it through various levels of the court system, to the Supreme Court, if necessary. In order to cover the costs of this work LEAF receives financial support from both public and private sources.

Since its inception, the organization has run an active fundraising program. Its ability to work for women's equality depends on donations from individuals and organizations. Charitable receipts are issued for contributions over $10.

LEAF has branches in every province and territory and invites individuals and organizations to become members and join in its ground-breaking work.

For more information, or to receive a complimentary copy of LEAF's newsletter, *LEAF Lines*, contact LEAF, 489 College Street, Suite 403, Toronto, Ontario, M6G 1A5.

Choosing Wines

Tony Aspler, wine columnist of The Toronto Star
and author of The Wine Lover's Companion

There is no such thing as the one perfect wine to go with any dish. Bacchus is not suddenly going to appear at your table and set about you with a vine stalk if you don't follow the recommendations you will find after many of these recipes. The suggestions I have given for wines to accompany the favourite dishes of Canada's leading food writers are merely that, indications of the type of wine that would marry well with the flavours of the ingredients.

Knowing that you don't want to drink fine wine all the time, I have given a two-tier choice — one for inexpensive, everyday wines that you would enjoy at the kitchen table and a more costly wine that you might choose when you are entertaining in the dining room. The choices are in broad wine styles which should be available at your local wine store. They go beyond the "red wine with meat, white with fish" homily and are based on the only real rule of pairing food and wine: the weight of the dish should equal the weight of the wine, that is a light wine with a delicate dish and a full-bodied one with a hearty meal.

But whatever you ultimately choose, remember that a glass of wine turns a simple meal into a gourmet experience. Enjoy.

APPETIZERS

From highly seasoned and robust, to light and elegant, appetizers set the tone for parties or the dinner to come. Often quick, sometimes colourful, but always characterized by a creative touch, this assortment of mouth-watering favourites will ensure that your evening gets off to a memorable start.

Smoked Salmon Pizza
Elizabeth Baird

Baird adapted this luxurious pizza from Sottobello, a Vancouver restaurant. We like it because of its ease — and you can use store-bought dough or your favourite supermarket pizza base or flatbread.

Elizabeth Baird is food director of Canadian Living *magazine and author of many cookbooks including* Classic Canadian Cooking.

Dough:

½ tsp	granulated sugar	2 mL
½ cup	warm water	125 mL
½ pkg	active dry yeast	½ pkg
	(OR 1 ½ tsp/7 ml)	
½ cup	whole wheat flour	125 mL
1 tsp	olive oil	5 mL
½ tsp	salt	2 mL
¾ cup (approx)	all-purpose flour	175 mL
	Cornmeal	

Topping:

4 oz	soft cream cheese	125 g
2 tbsp	snipped fresh dill	25 mL
½ tsp	coarsely ground pepper	2 mL
½ cup	thinly sliced red onion rings	125 mL
1 cup	shredded mozzarella	250 mL
1 oz	sliced smoked salmon	25 g

Dough: In large bowl, dissolve sugar in warm water; sprinkle with yeast. Let stand for 10 minutes or until foamy. Using electric mixer, gradually beat in whole wheat flour, oil, and salt until smooth, about 3 minutes. Using wooden spoon, gradually stir in enough of the all-purpose flour to make moderately stiff dough. On lightly floured surface, knead until smooth and elastic, about 10 minutes. Place in greased bowl, turning to grease all over. Cover with plastic wrap; let rise for 1 to 1½ hours or until doubled in bulk. Punch down; let rest for 10 minutes. Meanwhile, lightly oil 12-inch (30 cm) pizza pan; dust with cornmeal. On lightly floured surface, roll out dough to fit pan.

   Topping: Blend together cream cheese and dill; spread over dough. Sprinkle with pepper, onion rings, then mozzarella. Bake at 500°F (260°C) for 10 to 12 minutes or until crust is golden brown and cheese bubbles. Cut salmon into strips; arrange over pizza.

Makes 8 slices

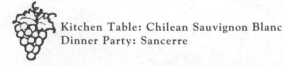

Kitchen Table: Chilean Sauvignon Blanc
Dinner Party: Sancerre

Tortilla Chips with Red Pepper Pesto
Rhonda May

Rhonda May lives in Vancouver where she is food editor of Western Living magazine as well as the publisher of Good Food, a quarterly newsletter that features the foods of the Pacific Northwest.

A fabulous, thick and savoury sauce that's a knockout with store-bought tortilla chips or an excellent topping on grilled hamburgers or baked potatoes. (Use the canned or bottled variety of red pepper that has had its outer skin removed by roasting.)

2 to 5	garlic cloves	2 to 5
1 tsp	salt	5 mL
⅓ cup	fresh basil leaves, roughly chopped	75 mL
4 oz	red pepper, drained and chopped	125 g
1 cup	fine bread crumbs	250 mL
¾ cup	olive oil	175 mL
3 tbsp	mayonnaise (optional)	45 mL
¼ cup	grated Parmesan cheese	60 mL
5 drops	Tabasco sauce	5 drops
	Freshly ground pepper, to taste	
	Tortilla chips	

Purée the garlic with the salt in a food processor. Add the basil and the red peppers and purée again. Stir in the bread crumbs. With the food processor running, pour in the olive oil in a thin, steady stream. Remove from the food processor into a small bowl. For a creamy dip, add mayonnaise. (If you think the dip will get long exposure to hot weather you may wish to leave it out.)

Stir in the cheese, Tabasco sauce, and ground pepper, and serve surrounded by tortilla chips.

Makes two cups (500 mL)

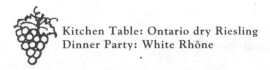

Kitchen Table: Ontario dry Riesling
Dinner Party: White Rhône

Chicken Pinwheels
Kay Spicer

With each slice showing off a swirl of filling, these appetizers are colourful as well as nutritious and tasty.

4	boneless, skinless chicken breasts (1 lb/500 g)	4
1 cup	finely chopped cooked broccoli	250 mL
½ cup	whole wheat bread crumbs (1 slice bread)	125 mL
1	small clove garlic, minced	1
1 tbsp	chopped fresh basil OR 1 tsp (5 mL) dried	15 mL
2 tsp	finely chopped walnuts	10 mL
2 tsp	soy sauce	10 mL
	Salt	
	Pepper to taste	
1 tbsp	rice vinegar OR lemon juice	15 mL
	Paprika	

Place each chicken breast between two pieces of plastic wrap; pound to ¼-inch (5 mm) thickness.

In bowl, combine broccoli, bread crumbs, garlic, basil, walnuts, soy sauce, and salt and pepper to taste. Evenly spread ¼ of mixture on each flattened breast. Roll up each piece from short end, jelly-roll style, tucking in stuffing. Brush vinegar or lemon on each roll; sprinkle with paprika.

Place rolls seam-side down on nonstick baking pan. Bake at 325°F (180°C) for 30 minutes or until chicken is no longer pink. Cover and chill. (Will keep, covered, in the refrigerator for up to 3 days.) To serve, cut into ½-inch (1 cm) slices.

Makes 24 slices

Kay Spicer is a home economist, food consultant, and writer; she has written several cookbooks including With Love From Mom — Real Home Cooking.

Kitchen Table: Chilean Chardonnay
Dinner Party: White Burgundy

Gravlax with Dill
Noël Richardson

*N*oël

Richardson runs

Ravenhill Farm on the

Saanich Peninsula on

Vancouver Island. From

her farm she supplies

herbs to restaurants in

Victoria and sells to the

public one day of the

week. Richardson is the

author of Summer

Delights: Cooking with

Fresh Herbs.

How about a delicious appetizer or first course that tastes like smoked salmon but is a fraction of the price? This excellent salmon "cooks" in its marinade in the fridge. You can use fennel instead of dill, decorate it with lemon slices, and serve it with toast points or buttered brown bread.

¼ cup	chopped dill	50 mL
1	fresh fillet of salmon (2 lb/1 kg) with the skin left on	1
3 tbsp	kosher pickling salt	45 mL
¼ cup	sugar	60 mL
½ tsp	freshly ground black pepper	2 mL
½ tsp	ground allspice	2 mL
¼ cup	vinegar	50 mL

Put half of the chopped dill in the bottom of a baking dish. Put salmon fillet, skin side down, over dill. Mix together salt, sugar, pepper, and allspice; pat over salmon. Pour vinegar over salmon and sprinkle with remaining dill. Cover baking dish with plastic wrap and chill in refrigerator with a brick on top of wrap for at least 24 hours. Spoon brine juices over salmon occasionally. To serve, wipe salmon clean and put on a wooden board, skin side down. Slice very thinly at an angle and serve with thin slices of rye bread or with crackers.

Makes 8 to 12 servings as an appetizer

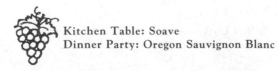

Kitchen Table: Soave
Dinner Party: Oregon Sauvignon Blanc

Smoked Trout Mousse
Bonnie Stern

This is a must-have recipe because you can serve it as a spread (try it on pumpernickel bread) or as a stuffing (it's great tucked into Belgian endives). Make it in a jiffy in a food processor or chop it by hand. Hand chopping gives a better texture. And lighten it up by using low-fat mayonnaise or unflavoured low-fat yogurt.

1½ lb	smoked trout (about 3)	750 g
⅓ cup	mayonnaise	75 mL
1 tbsp	white horseradish	15 mL
3 tbsp	lemon juice	50 mL
2 tbsp	chopped fresh dill	25 mL
2 tbsp	chopped fresh chives OR green onion	25 mL
½ tsp	freshly ground black pepper	2 mL

Fillet trout and remove as many bones as possible. You should have about 12 oz (375 g) filleted trout. Chop finely by hand or in food processor. Blend in remaining ingredients and adjust seasonings to taste.

Makes about 1½ cups (375 mL)

Bonnie Stern's Toronto cooking school has been an institution since 1973. The author of six cookbooks, she's a weekly columnist for The Toronto Star, a regular contributor to Canadian Living magazine and to CTV's "Canada AM" and CFTO's "Dini Petty Show." She is on the advisory board of Toronto's Second Harvest, a food recovery program.

If desired substitute another smoked fish such as smoked sturgeon, black bass, or whitefish for the trout.

Kitchen Table: Chilean Chardonnay
Dinner Party: Pouilly-Fumé

Bruschetta Pomodori
Iris Raven

$\mathscr{I}$ris Raven is a freelance food writer. As well as in Canada's most popular magazines, her work has appeared in several cookbooks. She has a regular column in Select Homes and Food.

One of the best-loved appetizers ever, this Italian dish is simple to make on a backyard grill. We like to serve it as an accompaniment to a main course, too.

2	large cloves garlic, chopped	2
¼ tsp	coarse salt	1 mL
⅓ cup (approx)	olive oil	75 mL
4	firm red ripe tomatoes at room temperature	4
8	large leaves fresh basil	8
	Black pepper	
1	narrow Italian crusty loaf, about 12 inches (30 cm) long	1

In shallow bowl, combine garlic, salt, and a few drops of the oil. With back of wooden spoon, crush to a rough paste. Stir in ¼ cup (50 mL) of the oil. Cut tomatoes into ½-inch (1 cm) pieces; add to bowl. Tear basil into strips; sprinkle over tomatoes. Season with pepper to taste, toss gently, and set aside.

With bread knife, halve bread lengthwise. Brush each half with oil. Place cut side down on medium-hot grill for 1 to 3 minutes or until golden brown. Remove from grill and place grilled side up on a large platter. Spoon tomatoes over bread; drizzle any remaining oil and garlic mixture on top, dividing evenly. Cut each half crosswise into 4 pieces. Serve immediately.

Makes 8 servings

Kitchen Table: Chilled Valpolicella
Dinner Party: Barbera

Jiffy Antipasto
Pam Collacott

Truly a quickie, and this microwave version also freezes beautifully. The recipe below feeds 18, so it's perfect served with crusty breads for a party. The combination of ingredients may seem strange, but the outcome is absolutely yummy. If you prefer, double the recipe and cook it on the stove over very low heat, just until the carrots are tender.

2	carrots, peeled, cut into ¼-inch (5 mm) rounds	2
1	small green pepper, chopped	1
½ cup	chopped celery	125 mL
½ cup	sliced mushrooms	125 mL
½ cup	chopped small white pickled onions	125 mL
½ cup	chopped marinated artichoke hearts	125 mL
½ cup	pitted black olives	125 mL
½ cup	sliced pimento-stuffed green olives	125 mL
½ cup	tiny fresh cauliflowerets	125 mL
1 cup	chopped sweet pickles	250 mL
1	7½ oz (200 g) can tomato sauce	1
⅔ cup	ketchup	100 mL
2 tbsp	olive oil	25 mL
1	6½ oz (184 g) can water packed, tuna, drained, flaked	1

Place all ingredients except tuna in a large microwave-safe casserole or simmer pot. Stir to mix. Cover and microwave on High (100%) for 5 minutes or until mixture comes to a boil. Stir, then cover and microwave on Medium-Low (30%) for 15 to 20 minutes, or until carrots are crisp-tender, stirring every 5 minutes. Stir in tuna and microwave on Medium-Low for 5 minutes more. Pour into freezer containers and freeze for up to 3 months or refrigerate for up to 2 weeks.

Serve with crusty bread and cold butter, or your favourite crackers.

Makes 5 to 6 cups

Pam Collacott is a home economist who has taught cooking to adults and children for 22 years. Her Trillium Cooking School is in her home 32 kilometres south of Ottawa. She's a weekly columnist for the Ottawa Citizen's food section, and a regular contributor to YTV's "Take Part."

Kitchen Table: Dry German Riesling
Dinner Party: Sancerre

Sun-Dried Tomato and Pesto Torta
Ladka Sweeney

Ladka Sweeney is a product developer for company brands with A&P. She ran her own catering company in Toronto for nine years.

We love this because, with its colourful layers, it looks as good as it tastes. It can be decorated with rosemary, parsley, or cilantro sprigs — or even tomato rosettes. A little of it goes a long way. This recipe will serve 15 to 20 people.

3 oz	package of sun-dried tomatoes (about 20)	85 g
1	jar basil pesto (½ lb/250 g)	1
1 lb	packaged cream cheese, softened	500 g
½ lb	unsalted butter, softened	250 g
	Box of your favourite crackers	

Pour boiling water over the tomatoes and soak for 5 minutes, then chop. Cut up cream cheese and butter; place them in a food processor, and mix until smooth. Line a large mixing bowl with plastic wrap. Place ⅓ of the butter and cream-cheese mixture in the bottom of the bowl. Spread chopped tomatoes evenly on top. Cover tomatoes with ⅓ of the cheese mixture; spread pesto over top. Finish with remaining cheese mixture. Store in refrigerator for up to one week. To serve, invert on a platter, then spread on crackers.

Makes about 15 to 20 servings

Substitute sun-dried tomatoes packed in oil, if dried are not available. Homemade pesto freezes well.

Kitchen Table: Valpolicella
Dinner Party: Alsace Pinot Noir

Spinach Tofu Dip
Rosie Schwartz

Whip this up in a food processor, and have it on hand in the fridge for snacking. Come party time, count this as one of the healthier dips around. It's tasty, so you don't even have to admit to the tofu in it.

1	package frozen chopped spinach, thawed (10 oz/300 g)	1
6 oz	tofu, pressed to remove water	180 g
2	shallots, quartered	2
1 ½ tbsp	Dijon mustard	20 mL
1 tbsp	lemon juice	15 mL
2 tbsp	light mayonnaise	25 mL
¾ cup	low-fat plain yogurt	175 mL
	Salt	
	Freshly ground pepper to taste	

Squeeze spinach to remove excess liquid. Process all ingredients in food processor or blender until smooth. Adjust seasonings.

Makes about 2 ½ cups

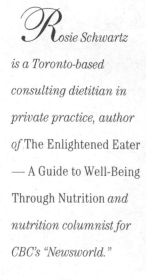

Rosie Schwartz is a Toronto-based consulting dietitian in private practice, author of The Enlightened Eater — A Guide to Well-Being Through Nutrition and nutrition columnist for CBC's "Newsworld."

Kitchen Table: Chilean Sauvignon Blanc
Dinner Party: Pouilly-Fumé

Endive with Chèvre and Shrimp
Anne Lindsay

Anne Lindsay is one of Canada's bestselling cookbook authors, having sold more than a million copies of Smart Cooking, The Lighthearted Cookbook, *and* Lighthearted Everyday Cooking.

This is easy to make and also looks great. Lindsay says she makes it the most often of all her appetizer recipes. The Belgian endive is fancy, but you can put the filling in celery or on cucumber rounds.

4	Belgian endives	4
5 oz	soft chèvre (goat cheese)	140 g
⅓ cup	skim milk ricotta cheese (6% M.F.)	75 mL
	Pepper	
¼ lb	small cooked shrimp	125 g
	Small sprigs fresh dill (optional)	

Divide endive into individual leaves; wash under cold running water and drain well. In a small bowl, combine chèvre, ricotta, and pepper to taste; mix well. Fill the wide end of each endive leaf with cheese mixture; top with shrimp and garnish with a sprig of dill.

Makes approximately 30 appetizers

Kitchen Table: California Sauvignon Blanc
Dinner Party: Sancerre

Asparagus Wrapped in Prosciutto
Rose Reisman

Sometimes you want a first course that's as unusual as it is delicious. This is one of those dishes — though once you taste it you'll agree that asparagus and prosciutto were meant for each other.

8	medium asparagus spears	8
4 oz	cream cheese (preferably herb flavored)	125 g
4	slices prosciutto	4

Heat oven to 400°F (200°C). Blanch asparagus in boiling water for 2 minutes. Drain and rinse in cold water. Spread cheese on each piece of prosciutto. Lay asparagus over top and roll up in the prosciutto. Set on baking sheet and place in oven for approximately 3 minutes, or just until hot.

Makes 4 servings

Rose Reisman, a former professor of marketing, is a self-taught baker who has written four cookbooks including The Dessert Scene — Toronto's Top Dessert Spots Reveal Their Secret Recipes *and* Pastas — Healthful Pasta Recipes from Top Restaurants.

Kitchen Table: Chilean Sauvignon Blanc
Dinner Party: Pouilly-Fumé

Baked Garlic with Warm Brie
Rose Murray

Rose Murray lives in Cambridge, Ontario, and is the author of many cookbooks, including Canadian Christmas Cooking, Secrets of the Seas, *and* Rose Murray's Comfortable Kitchen Cookbook, *her latest. She also is a food consultant and recipe developer, a broadcaster and contributor to several Canadian magazines.*

The way garlic changes its taste when it's baked long and slow still amazes us. It goes from sharp to sweet and nutty in a couple of hours. This recipe, which Bill and Nancy Schwarz of Cambridge, Ontario, shared with Murray, is for true aliophiles. Serve with crusty French bread.

4	whole heads garlic	4
¼ cup	butter	50 mL
2 tbsp	olive oil	25 mL
¼ tsp	dried thyme	1 mL
4 oz	Brie cheese	125 g
¼ cup	sliced unblanched almonds	50 mL
	OR filberts	
	Watercress sprigs	
	Light rye bread, sliced	

Cut top from each head of garlic just to expose tops of cloves. Arrange heads in small baking dish just big enough to hold them in single layer. Dot with half the butter, drizzle with oil, and sprinkle with thyme. Roast, covered, in 300°F (150°C) oven for 1 hour; uncover and continue to roast for another ½ to 1 hour or until cloves begin to pop out; baste every 15 minutes.

Half an hour before garlic is done, place cheese in small casserole. Melt remaining butter in small saucepan; add nuts and brown slightly. Drizzle butter-nut mixture over cheese and bake, uncovered, for about 20 minutes or until cheese is heated through but not melted. Cut the Brie into 4 wedges and serve each on hot salad plate with head of garlic, drizzle of oil from pan in which the nuts were browned, and garnish of watercress. Each diner dips the bread in oil, squeezes garlic cloves on top, and spreads with cheese. Eat warm.

Makes 4 servings

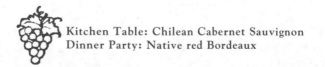

Kitchen Table: Chilean Cabernet Sauvignon
Dinner Party: Native red Bordeaux

Swiss Cheese, Garlic, and Black Pepper Spread

Ladka Sweeney

What could be more satisfying than this tasty recipe! As easy as one, two, three, four ingredients! All of them easy to come by and put together in a snap.

1 lb	Emmenthal cheese, coarsely grated	500 g
3 tbsp	Hellman's mayonnaise	45 mL
4	cloves garlic, minced	4
	Coarse black pepper to taste	
	Salt to taste	

Mix all ingredients together. Let sit at room temperature for 30 minutes or overnight in refrigerator, to develop flavour. Spread on crustless whole wheat or Italian bread. Do not heat.

Makes about 10 to 12 servings

Kitchen Table: White Rhône
Dinner Party: Chablis

Spicy Nuts
Cynthia Wine

Cynthia Wine

is restaurant critic at

The Toronto Star,

winner of three national

magazine awards, and

the author of five books.

She is currently working

on a sixth book about

eating.

We like making large batches and keep this on hand for snacks or to serve with drinks. It's also good as a garnish for soups or salads, or even crushed on chocolate ice cream.

2 cups	blanched almonds OR raw cashews	500 mL
3 tbsp	vegetable oil	50 mL
1 tsp	salt	5 mL
¼ tsp	ground coriander	1 mL
Pinch	ground cloves	Pinch
Pinch	ground cinnamon	Pinch
1 tsp	cayenne	5 mL

Heat a medium-size cast iron skillet over medium heat. Add the vegetable oil; when oil is hot, add nuts. Stir and fry for 3 to 5 minutes, or until nuts are golden brown. Remove nuts and drain on paper towels. Combine salt, coriander, cloves, cinnamon, and cayenne. Sprinkle over hot nuts. Mix well. Serve warm.

Makes 2 cups (500 mL)

Kitchen Table: Montilla Amontillado
Dinner Party: Amontillado Sherry

Fiesta Bruschetta
Judy Schultz

This has become as popular as pizza, though simpler to make. Try it as a side dish to summer grills or as a first-course to a casual party.

2 cups	chopped ripe tomatoes	500 mL
1	clove garlic, minced	1
2	green onions, chopped	2
¼ cup	black olives, sliced	50 mL
½ tsp	dried oregano	2 mL
1	large loaf French bread	1
2 cups	Monterey Jack cheese, grated	500 mL
¼ cup	Parmesan cheese, grated	50 mL

Heat oven to 425°F (220°C). Combine tomatoes, garlic, green onion, olives, and oregano. Cut bread in half lengthwise. Sprinkle halves with cheese. Spoon on tomato mixture and sprinkle with Parmesan. Bake 10 minutes.

Makes 6 to 8 servings

*J*udy Schultz *is food and wine editor of the Edmonton* Journal.

Kitchen Table: Barbera
Dinner Party: Barbaresco

SOUPS

Hot or cold, soups are one of the easiest ways to wake up tired tastebuds. These recipes run the gamut from sophisticated and exotic, to old-fashioned comfort food.

Cool Hand Cuke Cold Cucumber Soup
Fran Berkoff

Cold soups in the nineties don't need cream. So here's a delicious and refreshing soup that takes but minutes to make. Don't limit it to summer. For special occasions, garnish each serving with a few fresh salad shrimp.

½	English cucumber OR	½
	1 field cucumber	
2 cups	plain low-fat (2%) yogurt	500 mL
1	clove garlic, minced	1
1 tbsp	chicken stock granules OR 1 cube	15 mL
1 tsp	minced fresh dill	5 mL
	OR ¼ tsp (1 mL) dried dill	
¼ tsp	pepper	1 mL
	Fresh dill sprigs	

Peel about one half of the cucumber leaving some skin on; cut into 1-inch (2.5 cm) pieces. In a blender or food processor, combine cucumber, yogurt, garlic, chicken stock granules, minced dill, and pepper; process until completely puréed. Chill ½ hour or overnight. Garnish each portion with dill sprigs.

Makes 4 servings

rances Berkoff is a consulting dietitian/nutritionist in Toronto. She is nutrition columnist for the Toronto Sun *newspaper, food and nutrition columnist for* Images *and* Health Watch *magazines and co-author of the nutrition and fitness cookbook* Power Eating: How to Play Hard and Eat Smart for the Time of Your Life.

Double Mushroom Soup
Eileen Dwillies

Eileen Dwillies'

recipes and articles

have been published in

Western Living,

Canadian Living *and*

other Canadian

periodicals. She also

develops recipes for

corporate clients, styles

foods for magazine

advertising and

television commercials

and is the author of

several books. She is a

founding member of the

West Coast Culinary

Society.

Homemade mushroom soup is a perfect starter for a beef entrée. For a more intense flavour use your favourite dried mushrooms in the stock. Or use half fresh and half dried.

2 tbsp	butter	25 mL
1	small onion, chopped	1
1	clove garlic, minced	1
4 oz	fresh mushrooms, chopped OR 1 oz (30 g) dried mushrooms*	125 g
1 cup	chicken stock OR canned broth	250 mL
1	bay leaf	1
Pinch	salt	Pinch
	Freshly ground black pepper	
4	whole fresh mushrooms	4
4 tbsp	cream	60 mL
1 tbsp	Madeira OR sherry, optional	15 mL
	Parsley for garnish	

*If you use dried mushrooms, soak them first in warm water for about 5 minutes. Rinse to remove any sand. Strain the liquid and use with the chicken stock.

In a medium saucepan, melt the butter. Sauté the onion until tender. Add the garlic and cook another minute. Stir in the mushrooms. Add the chicken stock, bay leaf, salt, and pepper. Bring to a boil. Reduce the heat and simmer 15 to 20 minutes. Discard the bay leaf.

Cool the soup slightly. Purée in a blender. At this point the dish may be frozen, if desired. Otherwise, keep at room temperature for use within a few hours or refrigerate for use the next day.

Just before serving, slice the fresh whole mushrooms. Return the soup to the saucepan and stir in the cream. Reheat gently, but do not boil. Taste and adjust for seasonings. Add the sliced mushrooms and the Madeira. Garnish with parsley.

Makes 3 to 4 servings

Pear and Celery Soup
Daphna Rabinovitch

This is a mildly sweet soup that's perfect for a smart dinner party or an aprés-ski supper in front of the fire.

½ cup	unsalted butter	125 mL
¼ tsp	dried thyme	1 mL
4	large onions, sliced	4
2	bunches celery, finely chopped	2
6 cups	chicken stock	1.5 L
1 lb	ripe pears, peeled, cored, and sliced	500 g
½ cup	light cream	125 mL
	Salt and pepper	

In large saucepan set over medium heat, melt butter. Add thyme and onions and cook, covered for about 10 minutes, or until onions are softened and translucent, stirring occasionally. Add celery and chicken stock; bring to a boil. Reduce heat and simmer for 15 to 20 minutes or until celery is tender. Add sliced pears; cook until tender, 10 to 15 minutes. Purée in batches in food processor. Return mixture to saucepan; add cream and heat over low heat until heated through. Season to taste with salt and pepper.

Makes 6 to 8 servings

Daphna Rabinovitch is currently test kitchen manager for Canadian Living; she's the former senior pastry chef of the David Wood Food Shops in Toronto, where she co-authored The David Wood Food Book *and* The David Wood Dessert Book.

Easiest-Ever Tomato Soup
Julia Aitken

Julia Aitken
has been a food writer
for more than 15 years,
both in Canada and the
U.K. She was editor of à
la carte magazine, was
managing editor of
Canadian Grocer and is
now food editor of
Homemaker's magazine.
In 1986, Aitken
published her first
cookbook, Quick and
Easy Baking.

We like this when tomatoes are fresh. As it stores for up to three months in the freezer, you can get a taste of summer even in winter.

3 lb	ripe tomatoes, halved	1.5 kg
1	clove garlic, minced	1
1 cup	milk	250 mL
2 tbsp	brown sugar	25 mL
2 tbsp	milk powder	25 mL
1 tbsp	olive oil	15 mL
1 tbsp	Worcestershire sauce	15 mL
1 tsp	salt	5 mL
	Fresh basil leaves	

In large saucepan, combine all ingredients except basil leaves. Bring to boil over high heat. Reduce heat to medium-low and simmer, covered, 30 to 40 minutes or until tomatoes are mushy. Let cool slightly. In batches, process in food processor until fairly smooth. Rub through a sieve. Reheat; serve garnished with fresh basil leaves.

Makes 4 to 6 servings

Seven Vegetable Broth with Walnut Garnish
Marilyn Linton

You can use your food processor to make these veggies doll-sized in a jiffy. Or you can use a knife to mince them or slice some into rounds. The soup — light, simple, but elegant — is a welcome one for a lingering dinner party. For real luxury, add a dollop of (low-fat) sour cream and toast the walnuts.

4 cups	chicken stock	1L
2	large carrots, scraped and minced	2
2	leeks, white part only, thinly sliced	2
½	stalk celery, minced	½
1 cup	fresh spinach, chopped	250 mL
¼ lb	mushrooms, sliced	125 g
1	small red pepper, seeded and julienned	1
¼ lb	asparagus, cut in 1-inch (2.5 cm) pieces	125 g
½ cup	sour cream	125 mL
¼ cup	chopped walnuts	50 mL

Bring chicken stock to a boil. Add carrots, leeks, celery, spinach, mushrooms, red pepper, and asparagus. Lower heat and simmer 20 to 25 minutes. Ladle into soup bowls and top each serving with a dollop of sour cream and a sprinkling of chopped walnuts.

Makes 6 servings

Marilyn Linton is the author of several books, including The Maple Syrup Book *and* Just Desserts. *A former food editor of* Homemaker's *magazine, she is currently Life Editor of the* Toronto Sun.

If fewer calories, fat, and cholesterol are desired, substitute sour cream with either light sour cream or yogurt.

Creamy Squash Soup
Kay Spicer

Creamy goodness and gorgeous look and taste make this part of a perfect Thanksgiving dinner. It's amazing how quickly cooked squash turns into a smooth purée with the help of a food processor or blender.

3 cups	cubed butternut OR acorn squash	750 mL
2 cups	chicken broth	500 mL
1 cup	2% milk	250 mL
1 tbsp	low-fat yogurt	15 mL
1 tsp	chopped fresh sage OR a pinch of dried sage	5 mL
Pinch	cracked peppercorns	Pinch
	Salt and pepper	
1	slice dark rye bread, crumbled	1
1 tbsp	finely chopped walnuts	15 mL

In saucepan, combine squash and chicken broth. Bring to boil, reduce heat, cover and cook for about 15 minutes or until very tender. Purée in food processor or blender until smooth. Blend in milk, yogurt, sage, and peppercorns. Season with salt and pepper to taste.

  In small nonstick skillet, combine rye crumbs and walnuts; cook over medium heat, stirring occasionally for about 5 minutes or until crumbs are crisp and walnuts are toasted. Sprinkle over each bowl of soup. Serve hot or cold. (If reheating, heat to steaming but not boiling.)

Makes 4 servings

Corn Chowder
Jan Main

Main's grandmother made this soup and we loved it with oatmeal bread. As old-fashioned comfort soup, nothing beats it — especially on a blustery day.

2	carrots, peeled and grated	2
2	potatoes, peeled and grated	2
2	medium cooking onions, chopped	2
½ cup	pearl barley	125 mL
	Water to cover	
1	can creamed corn (14 oz/398 mL)	1
1	can 2% evaporated milk (13½ oz/386 mL)	1
	Salt and pepper to taste	
	Croutons	
	Paprika	

In large stainless-steel saucepan, combine carrots, potatoes, onions, barley, and water. Simmer, covered, until barley is tender, about 30 to 40 minutes. Add more water if necessary. Stir in corn, milk, salt, and pepper. Taste. Adjust seasonings. Serve garnished with croutons and a sprinkle of paprika. For best flavour, make the soup a day ahead of serving.

Makes 6 to 8 servings

Jan Main is a professional home economist who has run Jan Main's Kitchen, a personalized catering business and cooking school since 1978. She's a food writer and member of several food organizations, including the International Association of Culinary Professionals and The Toronto Culinary Guild.

New Age Scotch Broth
Marilyn Linton

We love the traditional recipe updated this way. This version uses no additional fat and calls for a garnish of chopped fresh coriander. Although the cooking time is long, the preparation (and cleaning up) is short. Make it one night, eat it another.

4 lb	lamb shanks	2 kg
8 cups	water	2 L
2 cups	beef broth	500 mL
½ cup	pearl OR pot barley	125 mL
3	leeks, white and green parts, chopped	3
2	diced parsnips	2
3	diced carrots	3
1	small onion, diced	1
	Freshly ground pepper	
2 tbsp (or more)	fresh, chopped coriander OR Italian parsley	25 mL

Place the lamb in large soup pot. Add water, beef broth, and barley. Bring to a boil and skim. Cover, reduce heat, and simmer gently for 1 hour. Add the leeks, parsnips, carrots, and onion. Simmer, covered, 2 hours or more. Just before serving, lift lamb out of broth, cut meat from the bones and return the meat to the soup. Skim off any further fat, add ground pepper to taste, and top each serving with choppped coriander. (Thin with a little beef broth if too thick.)

Makes 8 to 10 servings

Cauliflower and Bacon Soup
Barbara Mercer

This is "homey" in the best sense of the word. Satisfying and good for you.

2	medium cauliflowers	2
1 cup	chopped green onions (1 bunch)	250 mL
4 cups	milk	1 L
1 cup	water	250 mL
1 tsp	salt	5 mL
½ tsp	black pepper	2 mL
½ tsp	nutmeg	2 mL
1 lb	bacon	500 g

Barbara Mercer runs a tourist home, Gale Cliff, in Upper Island Cove, Newfoundland, which is internationally famous for its cooking.

Separate cauliflower into florets and cook in boiling water for 3 minutes. Pour cauliflower and water into blender and chop. Pour back into cooking pot and add all other ingredients except bacon. Dice bacon and cook until almost crisp. Drain bacon of fat. Add to cauliflower and milk mixture. Bring to boil. The soup might need to be thickened with flour and water paste depending on consistency desired. Serve at once.

Makes 12 appetizer portions

Split Pea Soup
Catha McMaster and Charlotte Empringham

Catha McMaster

is a nutritionist and

food writer, as well as

cooking school owner.

She has written three

cookbooks for microwave

and convection cooking.

Charlotte

Empringham

is a member of the

International

Association of Culinary

Professionals and the

Canadian Diabetes

Association. She has

many years' experience

in teaching and writing

about microwave

cooking. There has not

been a regular stove in

Empringham's kitchen

since 1983.

An economical and hearty soup that needs only a salad to complete it for supper. You can cut its usual lengthy cooking time substantially with this yummy microwave version.

10 cups	hot water	2.5 L
2 cups	green split peas	500 mL
1 ½ lb	meaty ham bone OR diced ham cut into small pieces	750 g
1	medium onion, chopped	1
½ tsp	salt	2 mL
¼ tsp	pepper	1 mL
1	bay leaf	1
1 cup	celery, cut in ¼-inch (5 cm) slices	250 mL
1 cup	very thinly sliced carrots	250 mL

Combine water, split peas, ham bone, onion, and seasonings in large casserole dish or soup tureen. Cover and microwave on High (100%) for 40 minutes, stirring several times. Remove bone; cut off meat and dice. Add meat, celery, and carrots to the soup. Microwave, uncovered, on High for 20 to 30 minutes, or until soup is desired thickness and carrots are tender. Stir occasionally.

Makes 10 servings

The Market Chowder
Kasey Wilson

This traditional seafood chowder with its West Coast flair is a meal in itself. Add a salad and your favourite loaf.

5	strips bacon, diced	5
1	onion, chopped	1
1	clove garlic, crushed	1
1	green pepper, thinly sliced	1
2	medium carrots, thinly sliced	2
2 tbsp	chopped parsley	25 mL
2	cans tomatoes (14 oz/398 mL), chopped	2
2	cans clam nectar (10 oz/284 mL)	2
1 cup	dry red wine	250 mL
1 tbsp	fresh thyme OR ½ tsp/2 mL dried	15 mL
	Salt and freshly ground pepper	
2 cups	peeled and diced potatoes	500 mL
8 oz	salmon, cut into bite-sized pieces	250 g
8 oz	scallops	250 g
6 oz	crabmeat	170 g
6 oz	shrimp	170 g

Sauté bacon in soup pot until crisp. Add onion, garlic, green pepper, carrots, and parsley and cook over medium heat for 10 minutes, stirring occasionally. Add tomatoes, clam nectar, red wine, thyme, salt, and pepper and bring to a boil. Simmer covered for 20 minutes. Add potatoes, cover and simmer a further 30 minutes or until potatoes are tender. Add salmon and cook for 5 minutes. Add scallops, crabmeat, and shrimp and simmer for 5 more minutes. Do not overcook. Serve immediately.

Makes 6 to 8 servings

*K*asey Wilson *is a food and wine writer, food stylist and advocate for food safety. She is also the author of* Spirit & Style: The New Home Cooking, The Granville Island Cookbook, Done Like Dinner: Tiger in the Kitchen *(with Tiger Williams), all published by Douglas & McIntyre.*

P.E.I. Lobster Stew
Julie V. Watson

*J*ulie V. Watson of Charlottetown, Prince Edward Island, describes herself as passionate about Canada's coastal regions, on both the Atlantic and Pacific side. Seafood is her specialty, and her cookbooks include Favourite Recipes from Old Prince Edward Island Kitchens, Seafood Menus for the Microwave, Barbecuing Atlantic Seafood, and Heart Smart Cooking on a Shoestring.

When noses tingle after a sleigh ride, there is nothing like this one-pot dish. Making the broth and preparing the seafood before we go out saves time, and we can be with our family and friends rather than in the kitchen. When we're ready to eat, the stew merely has to be assembled and heated up.

6 tbsp	olive oil	100 mL
4	large onions, cut into eighths	4
4	large green peppers, coarsely chopped	4
12	large cloves garlic	12
2 tsp	salt	10 mL
4	cans plum tomatoes (16 oz/500 g), cut into bite-sized pieces	4
6 cups	fish stock OR clam juice	1.5 L
2	bay leaves	2
1 tsp	black pepper	5 mL
1 tsp	coriander (optional)	5 mL
2 cups	dry white wine	500 mL
2 lbs	firm-fleshed white fish, cut into chunks	1 kg
11 oz	frozen lobster, thawed (1 can) OR 4 whole cooked lobsters, cut into pieces	320 g
1½ lb	mussels	750 g
2 cups	medium shrimp, cleaned (fresh OR frozen)	500 mL

Heat oil in soup kettle. Cook onions, green peppers, and garlic (mashed with salt) in oil over medium heat for 5 minutes or until tender. Add tomatoes, stock or clam juice, bay leaves, pepper, and coriander. Bring to a boil and reduce heat. Cover and simmer for 1 hour, until flavours are well blended and broth is slightly thickened. Broth can be set aside at this point and the stew finished later if desired. Add wine to broth and bring to a boil. Add fish. Cover and simmer for 15 minutes. Add drained cooked lobster meat, mussels, and shrimp. Cover and simmer 5 minutes until mussels open and fish flakes easily.

Makes 10 to 14 servings

Kitchen Table: Ontario Chardonnay
Dinner Party: Pouilly-Fuissé

Clam Chowder Supremo
Pierre Berton

Our families wolf this down with hearty garlic bread. Berton says that after skiing or shovelling a walk, this chowder's restorative powers are phenomenal!

2	cans butter clams (10 oz/284 mL)	2
1 cup	chicken broth	250 mL
1 tsp	thyme	5 mL
1 tsp	celery salt	5 mL
1 tsp	paprika	5 mL
1 tsp	freshly ground pepper	5 mL
2	large potatoes, diced	2
5	slices bacon	5
2	medium-sized onions	2
½ cup	dry white wine	125 mL
3 cups	milk	750 mL
1 tsp	Madras curry powder	5 mL
Pinch	cayenne	Pinch
	Salt to taste	
12	soda crackers	12

In saucepan, heat the nectar from the clams. Add chicken broth, thyme, celery salt, paprika, and pepper. Stir well. Add the potatoes. Reduce heat to simmer. In a skillet, fry bacon. Add onions, then clams. When onions are soft, add contents of skillet to the saucepan. Add wine and simmer until potatoes are soft. Stir in the milk. Add curry, cayenne, and salt. Serve with crumbled crackers.

Note: This chowder improves with age and can be kept for several days in the refrigerator.

Makes 6 servings

Pierre Berton works in all branches of communication: radio, television, films, newspapers, magazines, books. He has won three Governor General's Awards and two National Newspaper Awards.

Bistro-Style Lentil Soup
Kathleen Sloan

Kathleen Sloan has written about food for over eight years. She was associate editor at Goodlife magazine writing most their food features and restaurant reviews, and now reviews restaurants for eye, a weekly Toronto entertainment guide.

Lentils are really popular today but this exceptional soup is worthy enough for a formal dinner. Soak the lentils overnight for faster cooking.

1½ cups	dry lentils	375 mL
4 tbsp	unsalted butter	60 mL
4 or 5	slices lean bacon	4 or 5
1	onion, finely chopped	1
2	cloves garlic, finely chopped	2
3½ cups	chicken stock (fresh is preferred, but canned may be used)	875 mL
¼ cup	dry white wine	50 mL
¼ cup	sweet sherry	50 mL
1	bay leaf	1
¼ lb	salt pork	125 g
½ cup	table cream	125 mL
2 or 3	slices cooked ham, finely diced	2 or 3
¼ cup	chopped parsley	50 mL
2 tbsp	Armagnac OR Cognac	25 mL
¼ cup	heavy cream	50 mL

Cover lentils with enough cold water to cover them by 2 inches (5 cm) and leave to soak overnight. In a fairly deep, heavy saucepan, heat butter, add roughly chopped bacon and cook for 2 or 3 minutes. Add chopped onion and garlic and cook gently, being careful not to brown onion or garlic. Place drained lentils in pan, pour in chicken stock, wine, and sherry, and bring to a boil. Add bay leaf and salt pork. Cover and simmer gently until lentils are soft. Discard salt port and purée mixture in blender or food processor. Return to pan, stir in table cream, chopped ham, and parsley. Warm a soup tureen and pour in brandy and heavy cream, mixing carefully. Pour hot soup slowly into tureen and blend thoroughly.

Makes 4 to 6 servings

SALADS

Crisp, crunchy and nutritious, salads are usually low in calories and high in satisfaction. Many of these recipes can double as a main course, as well as fulfilling the role of appetizer, side dish, or perfect finish to a meal.

Michelle's Lobster Potato Salad
Michelle Ramsay

Try this for a different but wonderful first course or as a splendid salad for a special picnic.

2 cups	roughly chopped cooked lobster meat, fresh OR frozen	500 g
4 cups	diced cooked potatoes	1 L
¼ cup	thinly sliced green onion	50 mL
1 tsp	salt	5 mL
½ tsp	pepper	2 mL
⅔ cup	mayonnaise	150 mL
2 tsp	lemon juice	10 mL
2 tsp	horseradish	10 mL
1 tsp	dry mustard	5 mL
½ tsp	cayenne pepper	2 mL
	Romaine lettuce leaves for garnish	
	Hard-boiled egg wedges for garnish	

Place chopped lobster in a large bowl, reserving claws for garnish. Add potatoes, onion, salt, and pepper and toss lightly. In a small bowl, mix mayonnaise with lemon juice, horseradish, mustard, and cayenne, then pour over lobster-potato mixture. Toss lightly and adjust salt, pepper, and cayenne, if necessary. Refrigerate at least one hour. To serve, fan out romaine leaves on a platter or in a large salad bowl. Pile salad on top and garnish with wedges of hard-boiled egg.

Makes 6 servings

Michelle Ramsay is a Ryerson journalism graduate and a George Brown culinary grad. Although she lives in Toronto, she's the food editor of the London *Free Press.*

Kitchen Table: White Rhône
Dinner Party: Oregon Chardonnay

Warm Salmon, Fennel, and Potato Salad
Barb Holland

Barb Holland is The Toronto Star's *microwave columnist, a home economist and a national food consultant.*

This warm salad is an interesting combination of flavour and texture. The fennel provides both crunch and the subtle flavour of anise, and the salmon is a beautiful colour contrast.

Dressing:

1 tsp	Dijon mustard	5 mL
2 tbsp	white wine vinegar	25 mL
½ tsp	dried tarragon leaves	2 mL
½ tsp	sugar	2 mL
½ tsp	salt	2 mL
¼ tsp	freshly ground black pepper	1 mL
¼ cup	olive OR vegetable oil	50 mL
2 tbsp	chopped fresh dill	25 mL

Salad:

1 lb	small new potatoes	500 g
¼ cup	water	50 mL
2	salmon steaks (about 6 oz/175 g each)	2
2	sprigs fresh dill	2
2 tbsp	fresh lemon juice	25 mL
¼ cup	white wine, light stock, OR water	50 mL
1	fennel bulb	1
	Salt and pepper	
	Lemon juice	
	Lettuce leaves, for garnish	

To make dressing, whisk mustard and vinegar together in a small bowl. Add tarragon, sugar, salt, and pepper. Slowly whisk in oil. Stir in dill.

Scrub and halve or quarter potatoes (depending on size). Combine with water in a 6 cup (1.5 L) microwaveable bowl. Cover and microwave at High (100%) for 8 to 12 minutes, or until potatoes are tender. Stir or shake dish once during cooking.

When potatoes are tender, drain off any liquid and pour dressing over potatoes. Toss gently to coat completely, then cover and set aside.

Arrange salmon steaks in shallow, microwaveable dish with thicker portions towards outer edges of dish. Add dill, then pour lemon juice and wine over steaks. Cover and microwave at High for 3 to 4 minutes, or until salmon is opaque and firm to the touch. Set aside.

Trim leafy upper stalks and outer leaves from fennel and discard. Chop fennel coarsely. Remove skin and bones from salmon and flake into pieces. Gently stir fennel, then salmon, into potato mixture. Season to taste with salt, pepper, and lemon juice. Line 4 plates with lettuce leaves. Divide potato salad among plates.

Makes 4 servings

Kitchen Table: Chilean Sauvignon Blanc
Dinner Party: Pouilly-Fumé

Low-Cal Caesar Salad with Shrimp
Lucy Waverman

Caesar salad, created during the 1940s, enjoyed a wild comeback in the eighties. This version has a dressing with 46 calories per tablespoon (15 mL) instead of 120. This will ensure its popularity forever!

Dressing:

1 cup	low-fat cottage cheese	250 mL
	Freshly ground pepper	
2	anchovies, chopped	2
¼ cup	water	50 mL
¼ cup	skim milk	50 mL
2 tbsp	lemon juice	25 mL
2	cloves garlic, smashed	2
⅓ cup	olive oil	75 mL
¼ cup	grated Parmesan cheese	50 mL

Salad:

1	head romaine lettuce, washed and torn in pieces	1
6 oz	small shrimp, cooked	150 g

In a food processor or blender, process the cottage cheese, pepper, anchovies, water, milk, lemon juice, garlic, and olive oil until smooth. To make the salad, place the lettuce in a large salad bowl. Toss with half the dressing, reserving the remainder for another salad. Garnish with the shrimp.

Makes 4 servings

Lucy Waverman, a food writer for the Toronto *Sun,* Canadian Living, *and* Toronto Life *and a contributor to City TV's "Cityline," is the author of four cookbooks and runs a cooking school in Toronto. She is a member of many associations including The International Association of Culinary Professionals.*

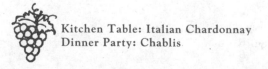

Kitchen Table: Italian Chardonnay
Dinner Party: Chablis

Oriental Chicken Noodle Salad
Marion Kane

Marion Kane is an award-winning writer who is food editor of The Toronto Star.

This is a great make-ahead meal and a nifty way to use up leftover chicken or whatever cold meat or seafood you have on hand.

Dressing:

⅓ cup	red wine vinegar	75 mL
¼ cup	soy sauce (preferably tamari)	50 ml
2 tbsp	vegetable oil	25 mL
⅓ cup	sesame oil	75 mL
1 tbsp	sugar	15 mL
1 tbsp	minced fresh ginger	15 mL
½ tsp	Chinese chili sauce OR your favourite hot pepper sauce to taste (optional)	2 mL

Salad:

½ lb	dried flat Chinese egg noodle nests OR pasta such as linguine	250 g
2 cups	cooked chicken, cut in chunks or strips	500 g
2 cups	bean sprouts, OR peeled and seeded cucumber, cut in strips	500 g
4 cups	shredded iceberg lettuce	1 L
4	fresh plum tomatoes, diced	4
¼ cup	chopped fresh coriander, cilantro, OR Chinese parsley	50 mL
¼ cup	raw whole peanuts	50 mL

Whisk together dressing ingredients, or shake in jar until blended. Add noodles to large pot of boiling water and cook until al dente (about 3 minutes for Chinese noodles, about 10 minutes for pasta). Drain well. While still hot, toss with half the dressing in large bowl. Cool to room temperature. Just before serving, add chicken, bean sprouts, lettuce, and tomatoes and toss with remaining dressing. Garnish with coriander. In a heavy skillet, toast peanuts over low heat for 5 to 8 minutes, or until browned, then skin and add to salad.

Makes about 10 servings as a side dish, 6 to 8 as a dinner salad

**Kitchen Table: Dry German Riesling
Dinner Party: Alsace Gewüztraminer**

Waldorf Salad
Cynthia David

Look at this old classic lightened up and you'll want to serve it as a luncheon dish, first course, or buffet table offering.

1	large firm red OR green apple	1
2 cups	roasted, cubed turkey OR chicken breast	500 mL
½ cup	pecan halves, toasted	125 mL
½ cup	thinly sliced celery	125 mL
½ cup	currants (optional)	125 mL
⅓ cup	finely chopped red OR white onion	75 mL
¼ cup	chopped parsley	50 mL
Dressing:		
½ cup	plain, low-fat yogurt	125 mL
¼ cup	light mayonnaise	50 mL
¼ tsp	grated lemon peel	1 mL
1 tbsp	lemon juice	15 mL
½ tsp	dry tarragon, crumbled	2 mL
¼ tsp	cinnamon	1 mL

Core and dice apple into ½ inch (1 cm) cubes. Combine with remaining ingredients in large bowl. To make dressing, combine all ingredients in small bowl until thoroughly blended. Pour over salad and toss to distribute evenly. Chill several hours to blend flavours.

Makes 4 to 6 servings

Cynthia David is a wonderful cook, a seasoned journalist, and food editor of the Toronto Sun.

Kitchen Table: Ontario Chardonnay
Dinner Party: Chablis

Goat Cheese Salad with Arugula and Radicchio
Mary McGrath

Mary McGrath is a home economist whose writing and recipes are regularly featured in The Toronto Star.

This truly is a special salad. Sprinkled with fresh garden herbs and topped with hot goat's cheese, it is magnificent.

Salad:

⅓ cup	extra virgin olive oil	75 mL
1½ tsp	fresh thyme leaves	7 mL
	Freshly ground pepper	
6 oz	fresh goat cheese, cut into 6 equal pieces	150 g
3	small heads radicchio	3
6 oz	arugula	150 g

Vinaigrette:

1 tbsp	Dijon mustard	15 mL
1 tsp	finely chopped fresh tarragon leaves	5 mL
1 tbsp	sherry wine vinegar	15 mL
1	egg (optional)	1
	Salt	
	Freshly ground white pepper	
½ cup	almond OR extra virgin olive oil OR a mixture of both	125 mL

In a bowl, combine olive oil, thyme, and pepper. Add goat cheese and marinate overnight. Use fresh parsley if thyme is unavailable. To make salad, wash radicchio and arugula. Pat dry on paper towels or spin in salad spinner. In medium bowl, whisk together all vinaigrette ingredients except oil. Add oil in slow, steady stream, whisking constantly, until dressing is thick and blended. Adjust seasoning. Toss greens with enough dressing to coat them lightly and divide among salad plates.

Heat nonstick sauté pan; add 2 tablespoons of the oil from marinated goat cheese. Sauté slices of cheese over medium heat for 30 seconds on each side, or place slices in oven at 450°F (225°C) for 1 minute. Top each salad with a slice of hot goat cheese. Serve immediately.

Makes 6 servings

Kitchen Table: Chilean Sauvignon Blanc
Dinner Party: Californian Fumé Blanc

Asparagus with Orange Vinaigrette
Cynthia David

We like this update of a simple vegetable classic. With its tangy vinaigrette, David praises this as a wonderful celebration of spring.

1 lb	fresh asparagus	500 g
¼ cup	vegetable oil	50 mL
½ tsp	grated orange peel	2 mL
¼ cup	orange juice	50 mL
2 tbsp	white wine vinegar	25 mL
1 tsp	Dijon mustard	5 mL
¼ tsp	salt	1 mL
Pinch	pepper	Pinch
3	oranges, peeled and sliced crosswise	3
	Lettuce for garnish	

Trim and cook asparagus until tender-crisp. Drain. In small bowl, stir oil, orange peel, juice, vinegar, mustard, salt, and pepper. Blend well. Pour over asparagus and orange slices in a shallow dish. Cover and refrigerate several hours. Remove asparagus and orange slices from dish. Arrange on lettuce-lined platter. Serve with remaining vinaigrette.

Makes 4 servings

Kitchen Table: Chilean Sauvignon Blanc
Dinner Table: Sancerre

Mom's Coleslaw
Edna Staebler

E̶dna Staebler, an

award-winning

journalist who lives in

Mennonite country near

Waterloo, Ontario, is the

author of several books

including Cape Breton

Harbour, Places I've

Been and People I've

Known, *and* Food That

Really Schmecks, *a*

Canadian cookbook

classic.

Who doesn't want a good coleslaw recipe? This one is not at all like the wretched sour stuff you get in most restaurants, says Staebler.

4 cups	chopped cabbage	1 L
1	small onion, chopped	1
½ cup	thick sour cream	125 mL
2 tsp	sugar	10 mL
1 tsp	vinegar	5 mL
	Salt and pepper	

Combine cabbage and onion. Mix the other ingredients together, pour the mixture over the cabbage and onion, and blend. If you want more nip, add a pinch of mustard.

Makes 4 servings

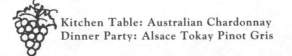

Kitchen Table: Australian Chardonnay
Dinner Party: Alsace Tokay Pinot Gris

Red and Green Leaf Lettuce Salad with Pistachios and Parmesan
Nancy Enright

Shell the pistachios at the last moment. It's worth the extra effort for this easy-to-make, delightful salad.

1	small bunch each red and green leaf lettuce (4 cups/1 L) torn	1
½ cup	shelled pistachio nuts	125 mL
1 tsp	Dijon mustard	5 mL
3 tbsp	balsamic OR wine vinegar	45 mL
½ cup	light olive oil	125 mL
2 tbsp	chopped fresh basil OR parsley	25 mL
⅓ cup	grated Parmesan cheese	75 mL

Wash and dry lettuce; tear into bite-size pieces. Arrange on plates; sprinkle with nuts. In small bowl or cup, whisk mustard and vinegar. Slowly add olive oil; stir in basil. Drizzle dressing over salad; sprinkle with cheese.

Makes 4 servings

Nancy Enright is a journalist and a consultant and recipe developer for numerous provincial fruit and vegetable growers' boards. She is the author of Nancy Enright's Canadian Herb Cookbook.

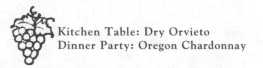

Kitchen Table: Dry Orvieto
Dinner Party: Oregon Chardonnay

Snow Pea and Mango Salad with Hazelnut Dressing
Rose Murray

Murray loves combining fruit and vegetables in colourful salads like this one with its nutty dressing. Hazelnut oil is available in specialty food shops, but you could substitute vegetable oil.

1 lb	snow peas OR sugar snap peas, trimmed	500 g
2	mangoes, peeled and thinly sliced	2
½ cup	finely diced red pepper	125 mL
Dressing:		
3 tbsp	fresh lemon juice	50 mL
½ tsp	salt	2 mL
¼ tsp	pepper	1 mL
3 tbsp	hazelnut oil	45 mL
3 tbsp	vegetable oil	45 mL
¼ cup	coarsely chopped toasted hazelnuts (filberts)	50 mL

In large pot of boiling water, blanch peas for 1 minute, or until colour is set. Immediately drain and refresh under cold running water. When cool, combine in bowl with mangoes and red pepper.

To make dressing: In a small bowl, whisk together lemon juice, salt, and pepper. Whisking constantly, add oils. Blend in nuts and pour over snow pea mixture. Toss gently to coat.

Makes about 6 servings

Terrific Tabbouleh
Marion Kane

We agree with Kane, who calls this the queen of salads. Experiment with it by adding more parsley or mint. Toronto vegetarian super cook Netti Cronish, who gave Kane a version of this recipe, recommends adding chopped seasonal vegetables such as zucchini, red or green peppers, or grated carrots.

1½ cups	fine OR medium uncooked bulgur	375 mL
1 cup	boiling water	250 mL
¼ cup	lemon juice	50 mL
¼ cup	red OR white wine vinegar	50 mL
2	cloves garlic, minced	2
1 tsp	Dijon OR other prepared mustard	5 mL
½ tsp	ground cumin	2 mL
	Salt and pepper to taste	
⅓ to ½ cup	good quality olive oil	75 to 125 mL
1 cup	cooked chick peas, drained and rinsed (optional)	250 mL
½ cup	finely diced red onion	125 mL
½ cup	chopped fresh parsley	125 mL
¼ cup	chopped fresh mint	50 mL
3	plum tomatoes, seeded, and diced	3
1	cucumber, peeled, seeded, and diced	1
	Fresh mint leaves	
¼ cup	toasted pine nuts	50 mL

In large bowl, combine bulgur and boiling water. Cover and let sit about 15 minutes, or until water is absorbed. Fluff with fork. In a small bowl, combine lemon juice, vinegar, garlic, mustard, cumin, salt, and pepper. Whisk in oil until mixture has thickened. Add to bulgur and mix well. Let sit in fridge at least 1 hour, preferably overnight, for flavours to mellow. To serve, stir in chick peas, onion, mint, parsley, tomatoes, and cucumber. Taste; adjust seasoning. Garnish with mint leaves and pine nuts.

Makes 6 to 8 servings

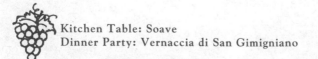

Kitchen Table: Soave
Dinner Party: Vernaccia di San Gimigniano

CHICKEN

Like a black dress and a string of pearls, chicken is a
classic. Roasted, baked, grilled, or sautéed, simply
prepared or lavishly adorned, we never tire of its
easy grace.

Italian Baked Chicken
Julian Armstrong

This make-ahead casserole looks as appealing as it tastes. If Armstrong serves it at a buffet, she bones the chicken so it is easier to eat. The pan juices taste delicious on fluffy rice. A salad of Boston or curly leaf lettuce is all you really need to complete the course — plus a good white wine.

5 lb (approx)	large broiler-fryer chicken, cut up, OR equivalent legs and breasts in serving-size pieces	2.2 kg
	Salt and pepper	
½ cup	freshly grated Parmesan cheese	125 mL
½ cup	fresh, chopped parsley	125 mL
1	clove garlic, minced	1
1 tbsp	fresh, chopped thyme OR 1 tsp/5 mL dried thyme	15 mL
½ cup	freshly made dry bread crumbs	125 mL
⅓ cup	butter OR olive oil	75 mL
¼ cup	olive oil	50 mL
½ cup	water	125 mL
½ cup	dry white wine OR dry vermouth	125 mL

Use a casserole with a cover, large enough so the chicken pieces can be placed in a single layer. Arrange chicken skin-side down, close together. On each piece, in the order listed, sprinkle an even amount of salt, pepper, cheese, parsley, garlic, thyme, and bread crumbs. Dot evenly with butter, and drizzle oil over all. Do not disturb layers. (At this point, casserole may be tightly covered and refrigerated up to 24 hours; bring to room temperature before baking.)

Carefully pour water down the sides of the casserole so it does not touch the layers. Bake uncovered for 1 hour at 350°F (180°C), adding another spoonful or two of water during baking so chicken does not dry out. After 1 hour, pour wine down sides of casserole so as not to disturb layers. Cover casserole tightly with aluminum foil and the lid. Bake another 30 minutes.

Makes 8 servings

Julian Armstrong has written about food for Canadian newspapers and magazines for 35 years. Currently food editor of the Montreal Gazette, she has won numerous food writing awards and has written A Taste of Quebec, a regional Quebec cookbook and travel book.

One way to cut food costs wthout reducing quality is to buy whole chickens. Cut them yourself into serving pieces (with kitchen shears or a sharp knife). Chicken costs approximately 10% more when pre-cut.

Kitchen Table: Orvieto (dry)
Dinner Party: Alto Adige Müller-Thurgau

Peppercorn Chicken
Elizabeth Baird

Lots of peppercorns and plenty of tangy vinegar mellow in this pleasing chicken barbecue. We like to serve it with a platter of sliced tomatoes and Spanish onions and slices of Italian bread, brushed with garlic and olive oil and toasted on the barbecue.

8	chicken legs (3 lb/1.5 kg)	8
¾ cup	balsamic OR red wine vinegar	175 mL
2 tbsp	olive oil	25 mL
2 tbsp	Dijon mustard	25 mL
5	large cloves garlic, minced	5
1 tbsp	coarsely crushed black peppercorns	15 mL
2 tsp	dried thyme	10 mL
2 tsp	dried oregano	10 mL
½ tsp	salt	2 mL

Trim visible fat from chicken; place chicken in glass bowl. In separate bowl, whisk together vinegar, oil, mustard, garlic, peppercorns, thyme, oregano, and salt; pour over chicken and turn to coat all over. Cover; marinate in refrigerator for up to 8 hours, turning occasionally.

Drain chicken, reserving marinade. Cook on greased grill over medium-hot coals or on medium setting, basting occasionally with marinade, for 20 minutes on each side or until juices run clear when chicken is pierced with skewer.

Makes 8 servings

If calories are a concern, use chicken breasts with the bone in, and without skin. (White meat has 192 calories per 4 oz/125 g; dark meat has 236 calories per 4 oz/125 g.)
If you do not wish to barbecue, broil in oven, basting continually.
Use fresh herbs if available. Taste is greatly enhanced.

Kitchen Table: Australian Petite Syrah
Dinner Party: California red Zinfandel

Chicken and Barley Cassoulet
Catha McMaster

*Barley is a wonderful grain that's too often limited to soups. This dish —
traditionally slow-cooked as an oven stew — is practically instant gourmet
thanks to the microwave.*

1 tbsp	margarine	15 mL
1	chopped onion	1
2	cloves garlic, minced	2
½ cup	chopped celery	125 mL
2	red peppers, chopped	2
½ cup	dry red wine	125 mL
1	can tomatoes (28 oz/796 mL)	1
1 cup	pearl barley	250 mL
3 cups	chicken broth	750 mL
3 lb	chicken pieces	1.5 kg
2 tbsp	chopped fresh OR dried dill	25 mL
2	green onions, chopped	2

In a 3-quart (3 L) casserole, heat margarine in the microwave on High
(100%) for 45 seconds. Add onion, garlic, celery, and red peppers.
Microwave at High for 3 minutes or until beginning to soften. Add wine,
tomatoes, barley, and broth to vegetables. Stir. Lay chicken pieces on top
of barley mixture. Cover with microwave-safe plastic wrap or a lid.
Microwave at High for 10 minutes. Microwave at Medium (70%) for an
additional 30 minutes. Let stand for 10 minutes before serving. Make sure
chicken juices run clear.

Makes 6 servings

Without a microwave oven, sauté vegetables in a large casserole
dish, just until soft. Add all other ingredients, cover and simmer
for 30 minutes or until chicken is cooked.

Kitchen Table: Alsace Pinot Blanc
Dinner Party: Alsace Tokay-Pinot Gris

Cranberry Glazed Chicken
Marie Nightingale

Marie

Nightingale compiled

Out of Old Nova Scotia

Kitchens *and, since*

1982, has written for the

Halifax Chronicle-

Herald *and* The Mail-

Star.

Cranberries are a familiar and favourite berry that grows wild or in cultivated bogs in Nova Scotia and Ontario. Since they're available from October through January only, we recommend storing a few bags in the freezer for dishes such as this family favourite.

½ cup	flour	125 mL
½ tsp	salt	2 mL
Dash	pepper	Dash
4 to 6	chicken breasts OR legs	4 to 6
2 tbsp	butter	25 mL
1 ½ cups	fresh cranberries	375 mL
1 cup	brown sugar, firmly packed	250 mL
¾ cup	water	175 mL
1 tbsp	wine vinegar	15 mL
1 tbsp	flour	15 mL
½ tsp	cinnamon	2 mL
¼ tsp	cloves	1 mL
¼ tsp	allspice	1 mL
¼ tsp	salt	1 mL

In a plastic bag, combine first three ingredients; add chicken and shake to coat. Melt butter in large frying pan. Add chicken pieces and brown slowly, about 30 minutes. Remove chicken from pan. Discard all but about 2 tbsp (25 mL) of drippings. To the pan, add cranberries, brown sugar, and water. Cook for 5 minutes or until cranberry skins pop. Mix vinegar with flour and seasonings; add to cranberry mixture. Cook, stirring constantly, until mixture thickens. Return chicken pieces to the sauce and simmer for 30 minutes.

Makes 4 to 6 servings

Removing all visible fat and skin from the chicken will result in a dinner that is lower in fat, cholesterol, and calories.

Kitchen Table: Dry Vouvray
Dinner Party: Condrieu

Persian Roast Chicken with Apricot Sauce
Allison Cumming

If a cook has a signature dish, this is the one people associate with Allison Cumming Gourmet Catering Inc. We know why: It's always a hit no matter how formal or informal the meal is.

5 lb	roasting chicken OR capon, boned — reserve bones for stock	2.2 kg
2	boneless chicken breasts	2
2 tbsp	butter, softened	25 mL
Stuffing:		
¼ cup	butter	50 mL
2	medium onions, finely chopped (approx 1 ½ cups/375 mL)	2
½ lb	dried apricots, chopped in quarters (approx 1 ½ cups/375 mL)	250 g
½ cup	chopped prunes	125 mL
¾ cup	raisins OR sultanas	175 mL
2	apples, peeled, cored, and diced (about 2 cups/500 mL)	2
1 tsp	salt	5 mL
	Several grinds of black pepper	
1 tbsp	dried tarragon	15 mL
1 tsp	dried thyme	5 mL
½ tsp	cinnamon	2 mL
Sauce:		
1 cup	unsweetened apricot juice	250 mL
1 cup	strong chicken stock	250 mL
1 tbsp	cornstarch OR arrowroot mixed with 2 tbsp (25 mL) cold water	15 mL
24	dried apricots, soaked overnight	24
	Fresh mint OR dill	

To make stuffing (it may be made the day before): Melt ¼ cup (50 mL) butter in a large skillet. Add onion, cover and cook on very low heat for 10 minutes. Add apricots, prunes, and raisins and continue to cook, uncovered, on low heat for 5 minutes. Stir occasionally. While the fruits are sautéing, prepare the apples. Add the diced apples to the other fruit and continue to cook for 5 more minutes, stirring occasionally. Remove from heat. Sprinkle salt, pepper, tarragon, thyme, and cinnamon over the fruit mixture. Stir very gently to mix together. Cool.

To prepare chicken: Lay the boned chicken skin-side down. Place the 2 chicken breasts where the flesh is thin. Heap the stuffing in the centre and shape it into a loaf. Bring the skin up over the stuffing and tuck in the ends. Shape to make a neat semi-cylindrical shape. Sew skin firmly together with a trussing needle and string. (Don't use nylon.) Turn the

Allison Cumming has her own Toronto catering service.

stuffed bird over, breast-side up. Pat it into an even shape if it looks a little misshapen. Place bird in roasting pan. Smear with butter. Cover and refrigerate until cooking time.

To make sauce: Mix apricot juice and chicken stock in a pan and bring to boil. Remove from heat. Mix cornstarch with cold water to make a smooth paste. Add ½ to 1 cup (125 mL to 250 mL) of the hot apricot juice and stock mixture to the cornstarch. Mix together. Return to pan with the rest of juices. Bring to boil, stirring all the time. The sauce will thicken and lose its milky appearance. Set aside until required.

To cook chicken: Heat oven to 400°F (200°C). Roast chicken in the centre of the oven for 1 hour. Baste regularly. At the end of 1 hour, remove the chicken from the pan and place on a serving dish. Keep warm. Drain excess fat from the roasting pan. There should be some dark drippings on the bottom. Place the roasting pan on a low heat. Pour in the apricot syrup/chicken stock mixture. Turn up the heat and bring to the boil, scraping the juices off the bottom with a wooden spoon. Boil for a minute or two. Add the drained apricots, cook just enough to heat apricots through, and then remove from heat. Serve some of the apricot sauce around the chicken and the rest in a separate dish. Garnish chicken with a few sprigs of mint or dill.

Note: The stuffing can be used inside boneless breasts, which are then wrapped in phyllo and baked in the oven.

Makes 6 to 8 servings

Do not stuff the bird until just ready to roast. Stuffing as little as 15 minutes in advance may cause health hazards. After the chicken has cooked, immediately remove the stuffing. Serve at the side of the chicken.

Kitchen Table: German Riesling Spätlese
Dinner Party: Alsace dry Muscat

Chicken Tikka
Julia Aitken

These traditional Indian chicken kebabs have a mild curry flavour that appeals to everyone.

1½ lb	boneless, skinless chicken breasts	750 g
3	small onions, peeled and quartered	3
¾ cup	plain yogurt	175 mL
2	cloves garlic, sliced	2
1 inch	fresh ginger, sliced	2.5 cm
2 tsp	chili powder, OR to taste	10 mL
2 tsp	ground coriander	10 mL
1 tsp	ground cumin	5 mL
½ tsp	salt	2 mL
1	lemon, quartered	1

Cut chicken into 1-inch (2.5 cm) cubes. Place in non-metallic dish. In food processor or blender, combine 1 onion, the yogurt, garlic, ginger, chili powder, coriander, cumin, and salt. Process until fairly smooth. Pour marinade over chicken; stir to coat well. Marinate, covered, in refrigerator at least 8 hours or overnight, stirring occasionally. Remove chicken from marinade. Thread chicken onto four metal skewers alternately with remaining onions. Finish each kebab with a lemon quarter. Barbecue on greased grill over high heat 5 to 7 minutes, turning frequently, until chicken is golden brown and no longer pink inside. Squeeze the barbecued lemon quarters over kebabs before serving.

Makes 4 servings

Debone the breast yourself for a fresher and less expensive dinner: place whole breast skin-side down. With knife cut white cartilage at end of breastbone. Bend the breast backwards. Carefully pull out bone, using your fingers. Cut through the centre. Separate the meat from the rib bones. Either leave as whole double breast or cut into two pieces.

Kitchen Table: Liebfraumilch
Dinner Party: Rheingau Reisling Spätlese Trocken

Gingered Turkey or Pork Scallopini
Iris Raven

We love the combination of ginger and turkey or pork. This simple recipe has great taste appeal and is colourful and healthy as well. You can decorate it nicely with scallion brushes.

4	green onions	4
1	carrot	1
1	stalk celery	1
⅓ cup	all-purpose flour	75 mL
¼ tsp	pepper	1 mL
Pinch	salt	Pinch
1 lb	turkey OR pork scallopini	500 g
3 tbsp	butter	50 mL
2 tsp	slivered fresh ginger	10 mL
¾ cup	chicken stock	175 mL
1 tsp	lemon juice	5 mL

Trim onions to 4 inches (10 cm). Cut carrot lengthwise into thin strips 4 inches (10 cm) long. Set aside. Repeat with celery. In shallow dish, combine flour, pepper, and salt; dredge scallopini in flour mixture and shake off excess. Reserve remaining flour mixture. In large nonstick skillet, melt butter over medium heat; cook scallopini for about 1 ½ minutes per side or until opaque and lightly golden. Transfer to warmed serving plate; cover and keep warm. Add carrots to pan; cook for 1 ½ minutes or until starting to curl. Add onions, celery, and ginger; cook for 1 minute. Combine stock with lemon juice; add half to pan and simmer for 2 minutes or just until carrots are tender-crisp. Transfer vegetables to plate with meat. Blend 1 tsp (5 mL) of the reserved flour mixture into remaining stock mixture; add to pan and cook, stirring constantly, until thickened and smooth. Cook for 1 minute longer. Through a strainer, pour sauce over meat.

Makes 4 servings

If turkey breast or pork seems to be tough, allow the raw breast or pork to soak in milk for 1 to 2 hours before slicing into scallopini. The result is more tender.

Kitchen Table: Dry Vouvray
Dinner Party: Alsace Gewürztraminer

Chicken with Lime, Ginger, and Coriander
Rosie Schwartz

We found this to be a chicken dish that's elegant enough for special guests but also easy enough to prepare for family meals.

1 cup	brown rice	250 mL
⅓ cup	wild rice	75 mL
3 cups	cold water	750 mL
Marinade:		
1 tbsp	fresh ginger, peeled and finely chopped	15 mL
1	clove garlic, minced	1
3 tbsp	lime juice	45 mL
2 tsp	vegetable oil	10 mL
4	single chicken breasts, skinned, boned, and flattened	4
1 ½ tbsp	vegetable oil	20 mL
2	red peppers, sliced thinly Salt and freshly ground pepper to taste	2
2 tbsp	coriander, finely chopped	25 mL

Put rice and cold water in a medium saucepan. Bring to a boil uncovered. Reduce heat to medium and simmer rice until all moisture has evaporated. If rice is not fully cooked, add more water ½ cup (125 mL) at a time and cook until grains are tender.

In bowl, combine ginger, garlic, lime juice, and vegetable oil. Place chicken breasts into this mixture and marinate in refrigerator for 45 minutes or overnight. Occasionally turn chicken breasts so that all sides are equally marinated.

In a saucepan, heat on medium-high heat 1 tbsp (15 mL) vegetable oil and cook chicken breasts about 3 minutes on each side. Remove and keep warm in the oven. Add 1 tsp (5 mL) vegetable oil to pan; cook red peppers on a medium-high heat for 5 to 8 minutes until tender but firm. Add salt and pepper to taste. To serve, place chicken on a bed of rice and garnish with red peppers and chopped coriander.

Makes 4 servings

Coriander or cilantro is known as Chinese parsley. If fresh is unavailable, do not substitute dried ground powder. Instead use ¼ cup fresh parsley.

Kitchen Table: Oregon Riesling
Dinner Party: Alsace Gewürztraminer

Crystal Fold
Kate Bush

*K*ate Bush
is a food consultant -
stylist who lives in
Toronto. She is co-author
of The Getaway Chef *and*
former editor of
Canadian Hotel and
Restaurant. *Bush is a*
regular contributor to
Toronto Life *magazine.*

Chinese food to take out is expensive but this dish can be the basis of an economical meal. Just add steamed rice and stir-fried vegetables. It's fun to eat, too.

Marinade:		
¼ cup	soy sauce (preferably tamari)	50 mL
1 tbsp	sesame oil	15 mL
1 tbsp	cornstarch	15 mL
1½ lb	boneless chicken breast OR pork tenderloin, cut in thin strips	750 g
1 inch	fresh ginger, peeled and sliced	2.5 cm
4	cloves garlic, peeled and halved	4
3 tbsp	peanut OR vegetable oil	45 mL
2	green onions, chopped	2
1 cup	julienned carrot	250 mL
1 cup	julienned celery	250 mL
1 cup	julienned green onion	250 mL
4 oz	rice noodles	125 g
	Oil for deep frying	
¼ cup	hoisin sauce	50 mL
12	iceberg lettuce leaves	12

Combine marinade ingredients. Mix well. Add chicken or pork. Refrigerate for at least 30 minutes.

Stir fry ginger, garlic, and chicken in hot oil until nicely browned. Remove chicken and set aside in warm oven. Add vegetables to pan. Toss and cook over high heat until softened, adding more oil if necessary. Add to chicken. Remove garlic and ginger chunks. Break rice noodles into 4-inch (10 cm) lengths. Deep-fry a few at a time in 1 inch (2.5 cm) of oil until they puff up (this will take only a few seconds per batch). To serve, each person spreads a little hoisin sauce on a lettuce leaf, tops it with deep-fried noodles, then the chicken mixture. Wrap lettuce leaf around the filling taco style. Kids tend to like it without the sauce.

Makes 4 servings

Kitchen Table: German Riesling
Dinner Party: Pouilly-Fumé

Chinese Chicken Salad with Sesame and Ginger Dressing

Lucy Waverman

We think this special chicken salad with an Asian taste makes a wonderful luncheon dish year round. It's also perfect on a buffet dinner table.

2 cups	spinach, washed and dried	500 mL
1	small Boston lettuce, washed and dried	1
2	green onions, slivered	2
1 cup	watercress leaves	250 mL
4	chicken breasts (4 oz/125 g each), grilled	4

Dressing:

4 tsp	soy sauce	20 mL
¼ cup	vegetable oil	50 mL
½ cup	lime juice	125 mL
2 tsp	brown sugar	10 mL
2 tsp	sesame oil	10 mL
2 tsp	finely chopped fresh ginger	10 mL
2 tsp	Dijon mustard	10 mL

Combine spinach, Boston lettuce, green onions, and watercress leaves. Place on a platter or 4 plates. Arrange chicken breasts on top.

   Dressing: In a small bowl whisk together the dressing ingredients. Drizzle over the salad.

Makes 4 servings

Use any variation of greens. The darker the green, the greater the amount of fibre. (Romaine, red leaf lettuce, and radicchio are other good choices.)
Substitute broiling the breasts with a light marinade of oil and garlic for grilling.

Kitchen Table: Vouvray
Dinner Party: Alsace dry Muscat

Cornish Game Hens with Lemongrass
Kasey Wilson

*Here, a traditional fowl gets a new treatment and the result is delicious.
Lemongrass is available at Asian shops or greengrocers.*

3	Cornish game hens, split in half	3
2 tbsp	light soy sauce	25 mL
3	cloves garlic, minced	3
3 tbsp	chopped fresh ginger	50 mL
4 tbsp	fish sauce	65 mL
4	stalks lemongrass, thinly sliced (remove coarse outer leaves and use the white portion at the base of the stalk)	4
	Juice of 2 lemons	
3 tbsp	sugar	45 mL
1 tsp	chili garlic sauce	5 mL
½ tsp	salt	2 mL
½ tsp	freshly ground pepper	2 mL
6 tbsp	vegetable oil	100 mL

Remove and discard giblets from hens. Rinse hens under cold running
water, drain well, and pat dry. Combine soy sauce, garlic, ginger, fish
sauce, lemongrass, lemon juice, sugar, chili garlic sauce, salt, and pepper
to make a marinade. Place Cornish game hens in a baking dish and pour
marinade over the hens, spreading it with the fingers to make sure the
hens are completely coated. Let stand at least ½ hour. Remove hens from
marinade and reserve marinade. In a heavy skillet over medium-high
heat, heat oil and sauté hens until brown on both sides. (If necessary,
brown the hens in two batches or use two skillets.) Transfer to a baking
dish (skin side up) and in a 350°F (180°C) oven, bake for 30 minutes or
until internal juices run clear when hens are pierced with a fork. Baste
hens with reserved marinade.

Makes 6 servings

If Cornish hens are unavailable, the smaller squabs or poussins
may be used. If none of these are available, substitute small
chicken pieces.

**Kitchen Table: Italian Chardonnay
Dinner Party: Sancerre**

FISH & SEAFOOD

As well as simple and elegant, fish and seafood are an important part of today's health-conscious kitchen. These recipes introduce some new and delectable touches to old favourites.

Papillote of Fish
with Carrots, Celery, and Leeks
Beverley Burge

This delicious, healthy, and elegant recipe is one of her favourites. In a 400°F (200°C) oven, the fish really do take only ten minutes!

2	medium carrots	2
2	stalks celery	2
1	leek, white portion only	1
	Unsalted butter	
4	pieces parchment paper,* each 12 by 18 inches (30 by 45 cm)	4
4	skinned whitefish fillets, each 6 to 8 oz (170 to 250 g) (OR use red snapper OR salmon)	4
	Salt	
4 tbsp	dry white wine OR vermouth	50 mL
	Fresh lemon juice	
4	sprigs fresh tarragon OR fennel OR parsley	4

Cut carrots, celery, and leek into julienne (very thin) strips. Place in small saucepan with 1 tbsp (15 mL) butter. Cook covered over very low heat 20 to 30 minutes or until tender. Cut large heart shape from each piece of parchment paper. Brush one side with melted butter. Place fillet on right side of each heart and sprinkle lightly with salt. Divide cooked vegetables into four portions and place on top of fillets. Add 1 tablespoon (15 mL) of wine or vermouth and a few drops of lemon juice to each. Top with sprig of tarragon, fennel, or parsley. Fold over left side of parchment heart, covering fish. To enclose, start at top of heart and make series of tight overlapping folds to seal the papillote until you reach bottom. Place packages on cookie sheet. In 400°F (200°C) oven, bake 10 minutes until packages are puffed and lightly browned. (If parchment packages are properly sealed, they will puff from the steam created inside.) For best effect, the packages should be placed on dinner plates and taken immediately to the table, where either you or your guests can slit packages open.
  *Parchment paper is sold at kitchenware shops and some supermarkets.
Makes 4 servings

Beverley Burge, a former instructor at London, England's Cordon Bleu, ran her own Toronto cooking school for many years prior to opening Brownes Bistro, one of Toronto's best restaurants.

Kitchen Table: Frascati
Dinner Party: Chablis

Whole Baked Fish with Rice
Julia Aitken

This dish is best when the fish is fresh. Garnished with sprigs of fresh dill, capers and lemon, it's an impressive buffet dish. Add steamed asparagus, or a combination of steamed or stir-fried vegetables, some whole wheat rolls and chilled full-bodied white wine, and you've got a special dinner party.

Stuffing:

1 cup	chopped onion	250 mL
1 cup	chopped celery stalk OR peeled and grated celery root (celeriac)	250 mL
6 tbsp	butter	100 mL
2 cups	cooked rice	500 mL
1 tsp	salt	5 mL
	Freshly ground pepper to taste	
Dash	rosemary	Dash

Fish:

1	5-lb (2 kg) red snapper, whitefish, OR trout	1
½ cup	melted butter	125 mL
	Salt and pepper to taste	

Stuffing: Lightly fry the onion and celery root (stalks need not be fried) in the butter and mix with the remaining ingredients.

Preparation of fish: Leave the head and tail on the fish but make sure the cavity is clean. Stuff the fish and secure firmly with toothpicks. Place in a greased pan, pour the melted butter over, and sprinkle with salt and pepper. Bake at 500°F (260°C) for 15 minutes. Reduce heat to 350°F (180°C) and bake 30 to 40 minutes longer. The fish is done when it flakes. Serve hot, with lemon slices.

Makes 8 servings

Steamed Mussels with Tomatoes and Fennel

Anne Lindsay

Cultured mussels, which require almost no preparation time, are now widely available, so this fast dish is perfect for a Sunday family dinner or a small casual dinner party. Low in fat, the combination of fennel with seafood is excellent. (If fennel is unavailable, use a drop or two of Pernod — too much is overpowering in flavour.)

4 lb	mussels	2 kg
1 tbsp	olive oil	15 mL
1	onion, chopped	1
4	cloves garlic, finely chopped	4
1	can plum tomatoes, 28 oz (796 mL), drained and chopped	
1 tsp	fennel seeds	5 mL
3 tbsp	chopped fresh parsley	45 mL
	Salt and pepper	
1 cup	dry white wine	250 mL
1	shallot, minced (optional)	1
2 tbsp	chopped green onions	25 mL

Rinse mussels; cut off any hairy beards. Discard any that do not close when lightly tapped or that are cracked. Place in large pot and set aside. In large skillet, heat oil over medium heat; cook onion and half of the garlic, stirring occasionally, until tender. Add tomatoes and fennel seeds; cook for 5 minutes. Add parsley, salt, and pepper to taste; mix well.

Meanwhile, in small bowl, combine wine, shallot (if using), and remaining garlic; pour over mussels. Cover and bring to boil; reduce heat and simmer for 5 minutes or until mussels open. Discard any that do not open. Pour tomato mixture over mussels; toss. Garnish with green onions. Serve in large soup bowls.

Makes 4 servings

Kitchen Table: Muscadet
Dinner Party: Sancerre

Seafood Casserole
Marie Nightingale

This east-coast seafood casserole is a favourite buffet-table dish. All it needs is rice and a salad for a complete offering.

4 tbsp	butter	60 mL
4 tbsp	flour	60 mL
½ tsp	dry mustard	2 mL
¼ cup	chopped onion	50 mL
1 tsp	Worcestershire sauce	5 mL
½ tsp	salt	2 mL
¼ tsp	white pepper	1 mL
4 cups	milk	1 L
¼ cup	white wine OR sherry	50 mL
1 lb	scallops	500 g
1 lb	haddock fillets	500 g
1 lb	cooked lobster (thaw if frozen)	500 g
2 cups	fresh, sliced mushrooms (or two 10-oz/284 mL cans)	500 mL
	Bread crumbs OR croutons	
	Parmesan cheese, grated	

In top of double boiler, melt butter. Add flour and mustard. Blend and cook for 2 or 3 minutes to remove raw taste of flour. Stir in onion, Worcestershire sauce, salt, and pepper. Gradually add milk, stirring constantly. Stir in wine and cook, stirring occasionally, until thickened (about 15 minutes).

Meanwhile, wash scallops thoroughly, removing the little part where it has been attached to the shell (it has a bitter taste). Wipe fillets with a damp paper towel; cut into bite-size pieces. Cut lobster into chunks. In a large saucepan, bring about 2 quarts (2 L) of water to a boil; add 1 tsp (5mL) of salt. Add scallops and simmer about 5 minutes. Add haddock and cook another 3 minutes, or just until it turns white and flakes easily. Layer seafood and sauce in a large casserole dish. Top with bread crumbs or croutons and grated Parmesan cheese. Put in a 350°F (180°C) oven until heated through.

Note: This casserole can be prepared in advance and refrigerated until needed. It also freezes well; thaw in refrigerator before heating.

Makes 8 servings

Kitchen Table: Australian Chardonnay
Dinner Party: White Burgundy

Seafood Creole
Susan Mendelson

In this version, time is of the essence and you'll have it on the table in no time flat. Spice it up, or down — as you wish.

Creole:

1	medium onion, chopped	1
1 cup	chopped celery	250 mL
½	green pepper, sliced thinly	½
3 tbsp	olive oil	45 mL
2	cloves garlic, minced	2
2 tbsp	flour	25 mL
1 tsp	lemon pepper	5 mL
1 tsp	thyme	5 mL
2 tsp	basil	10 mL
	Salt	
1	can tomatoes, 19 oz (540 mL)	1
1	can tomato paste, 5½ oz (156 mL)	1
1 tbsp	Worcestershire sauce	15 mL
¼ tsp	hot pepper sauce	1 mL
12 oz	scallops	350 g
6 oz	shrimp	175 g
6 oz	crabmeat	175 g

Sauté onion, celery, and green pepper in olive oil and garlic for 5 minutes. Add flour, lemon pepper, thyme, basil, and salt, stirring constantly. Mix together tomatoes, tomato paste, Worcestershire sauce, and hot pepper sauce; add to above, and simmer for 15 minutes. Add seafood and cook for 3 to 5 minutes. Serve hot. If you really like spicy food, you can add ½ tsp (2 mL) minced hot peppers!

Makes 4 servings

Susan Mendelson is a Vancouver celebrity and cookbook author, and is co-owner of The Lazy Gourmet, a gourmet take-out catering business.

Kitchen Table: Chilled Valpolicella
Dinner Party: Tavel rosé

Cod Steaks Provençal
Barb Holland

Buy steaks of even thickness for even cooking. This fresh and fast tomato topping is wonderful with the mild flavour of cod or halibut.

1 tbsp	olive oil	15 mL
1	onion, chopped	1
2	cloves garlic, minced	2
1	can tomatoes, 19 oz (540 mL)	1
2 tbsp	chopped fresh parsley	25 mL
1 tbsp	fresh lemon juice	15 mL
1 tsp	dried tarragon leaves	5 mL
Pinch each	salt and pepper	Pinch each
1½ lb	cod OR halibut steaks	750 g

In a 4-cup (1 L) glass measure, combine oil, onion, and garlic. Microwave uncovered at High (100%) for 2 to 4 minutes or until onion is softened. Meanwhile, drain, seed, and dice tomatoes. Add to onion mixture along with parsley, lemon juice, tarragon, salt, and pepper. Stir well and microwave uncovered at High for 4 to 6 minutes or until mixture boils vigorously and is slightly thickened. Stir once during cooking. Cut fish into serving-size pieces and arrange in a shallow dish with thicker portions towards outer edges of dish. Spoon tomato mixture over fish. Cover and microwave at High for 6 to 8 minutes or until fish is firm and opaque. Rotate dish as necessary during cooking. Let stand, covered for 3 minutes before serving. Season to taste with salt and pepper.

Makes 4 servings

Kitchen Table: Soave
Dinner Party: Alsace Pinot Blanc

Hot Salt and Pepper Prawns
Rhonda May

This is so good you might want to try it as an appetizer as well. When serving it as a main course, add steamed rice and steamed broccoli tossed with crushed peanuts.

1 ½ lb	whole, fresh, large prawns (in shells)	750 g
1 tbsp	Szechuan peppercorns	15 mL
1 tbsp	white peppercorns	15 mL
2	whole, dried small chili peppers	2
2 tbsp	coarse salt	25 mL
¼ tsp	Chinese five-spice powder	1 mL
1 tsp	sugar	5 mL
2 cups	peanut oil	500 mL
¼ cup	fresh coriander leaves, chopped	60 mL

Rinse the prawns, drain, and set aside to dry thoroughly. In a small skillet, combine the three peppers and heat, shaking the skillet until the peppercorns begin to smoke. Remove the pepper from the skillet and grind in a mortar and pestle or a spice grinder into a coarse powder. Combine with the salt, five-spice powder, and sugar and set aside. In a wok or a large, heavy skillet (preferably cast iron), heat the oil until nearly smoking. Fry the prawns in the oil for several minutes until they turn opaque. (Protect yourself from the hot oil by placing a wire splatter guard over the skillet as the prawns cook.) Remove the prawns from the pan and let drain on paper towels. Discard the oil in the pan and wipe the pan clean or heat up a second dry pan. Return the drained prawns to the hot pan and stir them vigorously for 1 minute while sprinkling liberally with three or four spoonfuls (or more if desired) of the ground pepper. You will not need to use all of the pepper mixture. Keep the remainder for use another time. Remove the pan from heat and toss the prawns with the chopped coriander. The prawns will taste best if served immediately, but if you intend to take them to a picnic site, wrap them in aluminum foil. They can then be eaten at room temperature or tossed onto a barbecue still in their foil packet or put into a boat oven for a few minutes to rewarm. Serve them in their shells and garnish with fresh sprigs of coriander and wedges of lime.

Makes 6 servings as an appetizer or 2 servings as a main course

Kitchen Table: Silvaner
Dinner Party: Aged white Rioja

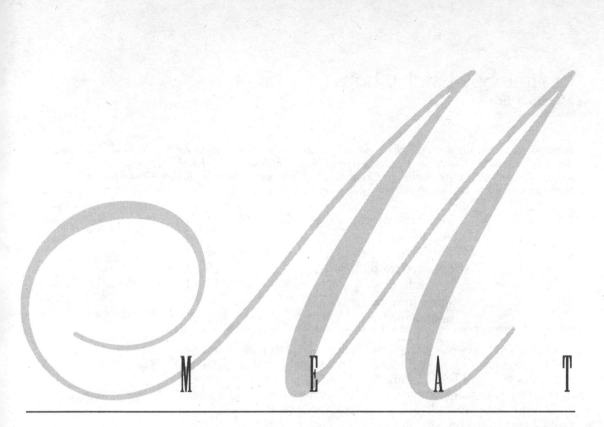

MEAT

Consider the lamb chop, the sirloin steak, or the pork roast. Where would gastronomy be without succulent cuts of juicy and tender meat? Here is a wonderful collection of tastes and textures that will stimulate your palate and inspire new heights of artistry in the kitchen.

Sesame Soy Lamb Chops
Margaret Fraser

Barbecue cooking, whether over charcoal at the cottage or on a gas model in the city, has become Canadians' favourite way to cook. This recipe, developed for the Canadian Living Barbecue Cookbook, uses a marinade that also works for chicken pieces, pork tenderloin, or turkey cutlets.

8	loin lamb chops	8
¼ cup	vegetable oil	50 mL
¼ cup	soy sauce	50 mL
1 tbsp	chopped fresh ginger	15 mL
1 tbsp	lemon juice	15 mL
16	sprigs fresh rosemary	16
⅓ cup	sesame seeds	75 mL

Place chops in heavy plastic bag; set in shallow dish. Mix together oil, soy sauce, ginger, and lemon juice. Pour over lamb; seal bag tightly. Refrigerate for 1 to 4 hours, turning bag occasionally. Soak rosemary sprigs in water for 30 minutes. Spread sesame seeds on waxed paper. Drain lamb and roll in seeds. Cook chops, each topped with a sprig of rosemary, on greased grill over medium-hot coals or on medium setting. Grill for 5 minutes. Turn and top with remaining rosemary. Continue to grill for 5 to 8 minutes or until desired doneness is reached.

Makes 4 servings

Margaret

Fraser is a home

economist/food writer.

A former food editor

with Canadian Living

magazine, she has edited

four of their cookbooks.

She's also the Toronto

Sun's *weekly microwave*

columnist.

For an intense sesame flavour, substitute 1 tbsp (15 mL) sesame oil for the same amount of vegetable oil in marinade.

Kitchen Table: Chilean Cabernet Sauvignon
Dinner Party: Red Zinfandel

Warm Lamb Salad Dijonnaise
Kathleen Sloan

This special salad serves six as an appetizer or two or three as a main course. The succulent lean and economical frozen lamb tenderloins now widely available marry perfectly with the greens and vegetables.

1 lb	lamb tenderloins	500 g
3 tbsp	Dijon mustard	45 mL
4	sprigs fresh rosemary	4
	Freshly ground black pepper	
1	sweet red pepper	1
1	sweet yellow pepper	1
2 tbsp	unsalted butter	25 mL
½ cup	walnut oil	125 mL
1 tbsp	tarragon vinegar	15 mL
1 tbsp	chopped parsley	15 mL
1 tbsp	Dijon mustard	15 mL
	Salt and pepper to taste	
2	bunches leaf spinach	2
2	bunches mâche (lamb's lettuce)	2
	Freshly grated Romano	
	OR Parmesan cheese	

Coat lamb with 3 tbsp (45 mL) of Dijon mustard. Pull leaves from rosemary and scatter over lamb with black pepper. Refrigerate lamb, tightly covered, at least 6 hours or overnight. When ready to cook, place on a rack over roasting pan in a 450°F (230°C) oven for 20 to 25 minutes. The meat should be medium rare. Put the lamb to one side and prepare the vegetables. Wash and seed peppers and cut into very narrow julienne strips. Heat butter in heavy saucepan and very lightly sauté peppers until just soft, about 10 minutes. Remove from pan. Prepare basic vinaigrette by whisking walnut oil, tarragon vinegar, parsley, Dijon mustard, salt, and pepper until blended. Wash and spin-dry greens and toss with enough vinaigrette to make them glisten. Arrange greens on large platter. Cut the lamb into thin, diagonal slices and arrange attractively across the spinach and mâche. Lay peppers across lamb in the opposite direction and freshly grate cheese over all. Serve immediately with freshly ground black pepper and warm crusty bread.

Makes 2 or 3 servings as a main course or 6 as an appetizer

**Kitchen Table: Australian Cabernet Sauvignon
Dinner Party: Red Bordeaux (Pauillac)**

Marinated Lamb
Barbara McQuade

Our favourite broiled or barbecued lamb is first marinated overnight in an interesting mixture of tart, sweet, and spicy. McQuade got this version from Ken Mounsey, owner of the Pink Geranium Restaurant on Galiano Island. And it is fabulous!

Barbara

McQuade is food editor

of the Vancouver Sun.

5 lb	leg of lamb, boned and butterflied	2.2 kg
⅓ cup	olive oil	75 mL
⅓ cup	fresh lemon juice	75 mL
1 cup	fresh mint leaves	250 mL
3 tbsp	honey	45 mL
1	piece fresh ginger, (2 inches/5 cm) peeled	1
4	cloves garlic, peeled	4

Trim all fat from lamb. Combine oil, lemon juice, mint leaves, honey, ginger, and garlic and blend until smooth. Place lamb and marinade in plastic bag. Marinate overnight in the refrigerator. Remove lamb from marinade and broil 15 minutes on each side. It should be rare in the centre. Slice thin to serve.

Makes 8 to 10 servings

Kitchen Table: Italian Cabernet Sauvignon
Dinner Party: Pomerol

Thai Beef Salad
Fran Berkoff

Yes, beef can be low in fat. This salad — with its incredible colours and textures — makes a great main course. Vary the vegetables to include favourites like asparagus or broccoli. Too spicy? Reduce the chilies.

5 oz	cooked lean beef (leftover roast beef OR steak)	166 g
⅓ cup	lime juice	75 mL
1 tbsp	minced fresh coriander	15 mL
1 tbsp	brown sugar	15 mL
2 tsp	soy sauce	10 mL
2 tsp	finely minced fresh ginger	10 mL
½ tsp	grated lime zest	2 mL
Pinch to ⅛ tsp	crushed chili peppers	Pinch to 0.5 mL
2	green onions, trimmed and sliced into long thin strips	2
½ cup	snow peas, sliced in long strips	125 mL
½ cup	julienned sweet red peppers	125 mL
½ cup	julienned unpeeled English cucumber	125 mL
½ cup	bean sprouts	125 mL
⅓ cup	red onion, thinly sliced	75 mL
1 tbsp	coarsely chopped unsalted peanuts Fresh coriander sprigs	15 mL

Slice beef into ¼-inch (1 cm) slices and then cut into long narrow strips. In small shallow dish, mix lime juice, coriander, sugar, soy sauce, ginger, lime zest, and chili peppers; add beef strips to mixture; cover and marinate about 30 minutes at room temperature or overnight in refrigerator. In large bowl, combine green onions, snow peas, peppers, cucumber, bean sprouts, and onion; add beef and marinade to vegetables. Toss to coat. Sprinkle peanuts over and garnish with coriander.

Makes 2 servings

Kitchen Table: Red Rhône
Dinner Party: Amarone

Pierre's Pepper Steak
Pierre Berton

This is a cooking classic that's fun to make as well as eat. Berton likes to make it in a pan at tableside for an intimate dinner party.

4 tbsp	butter	50 mL
4	onions, finely chopped	4
	Cracked black pepper	
4	steak filets (6 to 8 oz/150 to 250 g), cut 1 ¼ inches (3 cm) thick	4
1 cup	red wine	250 mL
¼ cup	brandy	50 mL

In skillet, melt butter. Sauté onions until soft. Set aside. Press black pepper into both sides and the edge of the meat. In a clean hot skillet, sear steaks on both sides and cook until half done. Cover with onions and add red wine. Complete cooking steaks to personal taste. (I insist on rare.) In small skillet, warm the brandy and flame. Pour over steaks and serve.

  Note: This piquant dish can be served with a chilled salad and any light fruit dessert.

Makes 4 servings

Kitchen Table: Greek red
Dinner Party: Red Zinfandel

Judith's Flank Steak
Judith Finlayson

*J*udith Finlayson has been called "one of the leading feminist writers in North America" and most people associate her name with her many articles and columns on women. Few remember that she started her career as a food writer and a cook. Her recipes, restaurant reviews, and articles on culinary subjects have appeared in many Canadian magazines including Maclean's, Chatelaine, Toronto Life, *and* Quest.

This is a knockout with everyone, outstanding on the barbecue, and even excellent cold! Dijon or flavoured mustard makes an excellent accompaniment.

2	cloves garlic, coarsely chopped (add more if desired)	2
1	small onion, coarsely chopped	1
2	fresh chili peppers, coarsely chopped	2
1 tsp	grated fresh ginger	5 mL
3 tbsp	lemon juice	45 mL
¾ cup	Japanese soy sauce	175 mL
1	whole flank steak	1

Whisk all ingredients, except for the steak, in a blender or food processor until liquified. Pour mixture over meat, cover, and marinate overnight in the refrigerator, turning several times. Bring to room temperature and grill on barbecue or in the oven to desired degree of doneness.

  Note: Japanese soy sauce, which is lighter and less salty than the Chinese version, is essential.

Makes 4 servings

Kitchen Table: Australian Shiraz
Dinner Party: Mature Barolo

Peppery Pot Roast
Rose Murray

This comforting one-dish meal has the added bonus of an intriguing sauce, no added fat, and, best of all, takes little effort. Use homemade or canned stock, not powdered concentrate.

1	chuck OR blade beef roast (4 lb/2 kg)	1
1	can tomato sauce (28 oz/796 mL)	1
2½ cups	beef stock	625 mL
1 cup	dry red wine	250 mL
¼ cup	low-salt soy sauce	50 mL
2 tbsp	packed brown sugar	25 mL
2	bay leaves	2
½ tsp	hot pepper flakes	2 mL
½ tsp	pepper	2 mL
1	whole head garlic, separated into cloves and peeled	1
1	butternut squash, peeled and cut in large pieces	1
6 to 8	potatoes, peeled	6 to 8
6 to 8	wedges green cabbage	6 to 8

Place roast in very large roasting pan. In large bowl, stir together tomato sauce, beef stock, wine, soy sauce, sugar, bay leaves, hot pepper flakes, and pepper; pour over roast. Add garlic. Cover and roast at 325°F (160°C) for 1½ hours. Add squash, potatoes, and cabbage; cover and roast for 1 to 1½ hours or until meat and vegetables are very tender. Remove meat and vegetables to heated platter; cover and set aside to keep warm. Remove bay leaves. Boil liquid in pan until desired consistency for sauce, 5 to 10 minutes. Slice beef and pass sauce in heated sauceboat.

Makes 6 to 8 servings

Kitchen Table: Red Côtes-du-Rhône
Dinner Party: California Syrah

French Veal Stew
Joanne Kates

*oanne Kates,
an award-winning food
writer and author of
several books, is
restaurant critic for
The Globe and Mail.*

This is a great Sunday dinner and a fine classic dish. You just cannot do better. Serve with steamed rice and green beans sautéed in garlic butter.

1 ½ lb	stewing veal cut into bite-size pieces	750 g
9 tbsp	butter	135 mL
3	onions	3
6	carrots	6
4 tbsp	flour	60 mL
1	bouquet garni (made from 10 sprigs parsley, 1 bay leaf, and 1 stalk of celery cut into thirds, tied together with string)	1
3 cups	beef OR chicken stock OR vegetable water	750 mL
3	cloves garlic, diced	3
1 tbsp	tomato paste	15 mL
¼ tsp	thyme	1 mL
1 cup	white wine	250 mL
½ lb	mushrooms	250 g
	Salt and pepper to taste	

In heavy-bottomed pan, on high heat, fry the veal in 3 tbsp (45 mL) of the butter, turning the pieces so that they brown on both top and bottom — the meat must be very well browned (close to burnt) in order to establish a flavour foundation for the stew. After the meat is well browned, transfer it to the stew pot. Dice the onions, brown them in 2 tbsp (30 mL) of the butter, and add to the stew pot. Slice the carrots, brown them well, and add to the stew pot. Add 3 more tbsp (45 mL) butter to the frying pan and stir in the flour. Stir over the heat for about 3 minutes, to brown the flour and avoid a floury taste. Add the butter and flour to the stew pot. Add the bouquet garni, stock or water, diced garlic, tomato paste, thyme, and white wine to the pot. Bring the stew to a simmer (do not boil or it will toughen) and cook 1 hour. Slice the mushrooms and fry them in the remaining 1 tbsp (15 mL) butter on high heat for 2 minutes. Set aside. Just before serving, add the mushrooms and salt and pepper.

Makes 4 servings

Kitchen Table: Valpolicella
Dinner Party: Red Burgundy

Chili Casserole with Polenta
Iris Raven

Family and guests love this modern-day chili. Even though it has a healthy proportion of vegetables to meat, it is every bit as satisfying as the traditional meatier version. The polenta topping gives it an up-to-date appeal.

1 lb	lean beef	500 g
2 tbsp	all-purpose flour	25 mL
	Salt and pepper	
2 tbsp	vegetable oil	30 mL
2 cups	onion, coarsely chopped	500 mL
2	cloves garlic, minced	2
1	small sweet red pepper, seeded and chopped	1
1 cup	finely diced carrots	250 mL
1 cup	coarsely chopped cabbage	250 mL
2 tbsp	chili powder	25 mL
1 tsp	dried oregano	5 mL
¼ tsp	cinnamon	1 mL
¼ tsp	red pepper flakes	1 mL
1	can tomatoes (28 oz/796 mL)	1
1	can red kidney beans (28 oz/796 mL), drained	1
	Polenta (recipe follows)	

Trim away any fat and cut beef into 1-inch (2.5 cm) pieces. In shallow dish, season flour with salt and pepper. Add beef and toss until flour is taken up; set aside. In large nonstick skillet, heat 1 tbsp (15 mL) of the oil over medium heat; cook onions, garlic, and red pepper, stirring, until onions are translucent. Add carrots and cabbage; cook, stirring, for 2 minutes. Transfer to 10-cup (2.5 L) casserole dish; stir in chili powder, oregano, cinnamon, and red pepper flakes. Set aside. Heat remaining oil in skillet over medium-high heat; cook meat, in batches, turning to brown on all sides. Add to casserole. Break up tomatoes; stir into casserole. Cover and bake at 325°F (160°C) for 1½ hours or until meat is tender, stirring twice during cooking. Taste and season with salt, if required, and pepper. Stir in beans. (Recipe can be prepared to this point, cooled, covered, and refrigerated for up to 2 days or frozen. Thaw overnight in refrigerator before continuing and increase final cooking time by 10 minutes.)

Polenta

3 cups	water	750 mL
¾ cup	cornmeal	175 mL
1 tbsp	butter	15 mL
½ tsp	salt	2 mL

In small saucepan, combine water, cornmeal, butter, and salt; let stand for 10 minutes. Bring to boil, stirring constantly; reduce heat to medium-low and cook, stirring frequently, for 12 to 15 minutes or until spoon drawn through mixture leaves a line. Pour into nonstick 8-inch (1.2 L) round cake pan. Let cool and refrigerate for at least 30 minutes or, when completely cold, cover and refrigerate for up to 2 days.

Cut polenta into wedges; arrange on top of chili. Bake for 20 to 25 minutes or until polenta is lightly golden on top.

Makes 6 servings

Kitchen Table: Chianti
Dinner Table: Crozes-Hermitage

Loin of Veal with Green Apple Sauce
Rollande DesBois

This could be your house veal roast. It's special, tasty, a little different, and welcome as either a Sunday family dinner or a special party dish.

2 lb	loin of veal, boned	1 kg
1 tbsp	oil	15 mL
1 tbsp	butter	15 mL
1	onion, diced	1
1	clove garlic	1
1	carrot, chopped	1
½ cup	35% cream	125 mL
½ cup	water	125 mL
½ cup	white wine	125 mL
	Salt and ground pepper	

Sauce:

	Meat juice from cooked veal	
1	Granny Smith apple	1
	Juice of ½ lemon	
2 tbsp	butter	30 mL
	Salt and pepper	
1 tsp	sugar	5 mL

Accompaniment:

1 ¼ lb	red potatoes, cooked with skins on	625 g
	Salt and pepper	
Pinch	curry powder	Pinch
Pinch	cinnamon	Pinch
Pinch	paprika	Pinch
1 cup	35% cream	200 mL

Rollande DesBois trained at the Cordon Bleu Cookery School in London, England, and continued her training with some of France's best-known chefs. She has contributed articles and recipes to various magazines, including Chatelaine, *and is the author of* La Fine Cuisine Québécoise. *It was reissued under the title,* La Fine Cuisine de Rollande DesBois, *in 1988.*

In skillet, brown veal in oil and butter. Add onion, garlic, and carrot. Let cook for several minutes. Transfer the veal and the vegetables into a roasting pan (reserve the skillet for cooking potatoes), add cream, water, wine, salt, and pepper. Cover and roast in the oven at 350°F (180°C) for 60 to 70 minutes. Baste the veal 4 or 5 times during roasting. Remove cover for the last 15 minutes. When done, remove the veal from the roasting pan, cover, and let stand for 10 minutes before slicing.

Sauce: Put the sauce (left over from cooking the veal) through a strainer, skim off the fat, and reduce slightly. To make it smoother, blend it in an electric mixer for 45 seconds. Cut the unpeeled apple into small cubes, moisten with lemon juice, and cook in butter. Add salt, pepper, and sugar. Drain the apple cubes, and add them to the sauce. Taste for seasonings. Slice the veal, and serve with potatoes and apple sauce.

Accompaniment: Peel cooked potatoes while still warm and arrange them on an ovenproof dish. Add salt and pepper. Add a pinch each of curry powder, cinnamon, and paprika to cream, coat the potatoes with this mixture, and cover with aluminum foil. Put into the oven at the same time as the veal and cook for 20 to 30 minutes, stirring from time to time. When the potatoes are cooked, the cream should be reduced and should coat each piece of potato. Keep hot until ready to serve.

Makes 6 to 8 servings

Kitchen Table: Beaujolais
Dinner Party: Alsace Pinot Noir

Endives and Ham "Gratinés"

Suzanne Leclerc

Try this neat luncheon dish for its simplicity and versatility. Experiment with your favourite ham — prosciutto or Westphalian.

8 to 10	endives	8 to 10
	Salt and pepper	
2 tbsp	lemon juice	30 mL
2 tbsp	butter	30 mL
¼ cup	white wine OR chicken broth	60 mL
	OR boiling water	
8 to 10	thin slices of ham	8 to 10
2 cups	Mornay sauce (cheese	500 mL
	Béchamel sauce)	
¼ cup	grated cheese,	50 mL
	Gruyère OR Emmental	

Butter a flame-proof casserole. Trim the endives. Arrange the whole endives in two layers. Season with salt, pepper, and lemon juice. Dot with butter. Pour in the liquid. Cover and simmer 10 minutes. Drain and press the endives. Wrap each endive in a thin slice of ham. Arrange them in a buttered baking dish. Pour over some Mornay sauce. Sprinkle with grated cheese. Bake in upper third of oven at 375°F (190°C) for about 20 minutes or until top is nicely browned.

Makes 4 to 5 servings

Mornay Sauce

4 tbsp	unsalted butter (½ stick)	60 mL
3 tbsp	unbleached all-purpose flour	45 mL
1 ½ cups	milk	375 mL
⅓ cup	grated Gruyère cheese	75 mL
	Paprika	
	Ground nutmeg	
	Salt and ground white pepper, to taste	

Melt the butter in a heavy saucepan. Add the flour and cook, stirring, over low heat for 3 minutes. Raise the heat to medium and slowly add the milk, stirring constantly with a wire whisk. Continue whisking until the sauce begins to thicken, about 3 minutes. Slowly sprinkle in the Gruyère, stirring as you add it. When all the cheese has been added and has melted, add a pinch of paprika, nutmeg, and salt and white pepper. Stir well, and remove from the heat.

Makes about 2 cups (500 mL)

Kitchen Table: Chilean Chardonnay
Dinner Party: Pouilly-Fumé

Suzanne Leclerc is a food specialist with the Agriculture Department of the government of Quebec. For twenty years she has been developing recipes for and promoting the newest Quebec food products.

Pork Tenderloin
with Morels and Madeira
Joanne Kates

Kates keeps dried morels soaking in Madeira in a small jar in the fridge so she can pull them out in a hurry and make this dish when she's looking for something glamorous. We like her version of "instant gourmet."

1 oz	dried morels OR porcini OR any other dried wild mushroom	30 g
1½ cups	Madeira OR port wine	375 mL
1½ lb	pork tenderloin	750 g
3 tbsp	flour seasoned with salt and pepper	45 mL
3 tbsp	butter	45 mL
3	shallots OR the white part of 3 green onions	3
1 cup	whipping cream	250 mL
¼ tsp	dried thyme OR ½ tsp/2 mL chopped fresh thyme	1 mL

Put the dried mushrooms in a small jar with the Madeira, and leave to soak in the fridge overnight (they may be left much longer — they keep indefinitely in the fridge).

Heat oven to 300°F (150°C). Cut the pork into thin slices, about ½-inch (1 cm) thick. Dredge the pork with seasoned flour and take care to shake off all the excess flour. Fry the pork in the butter until barely cooked, about 3 minutes per side. Remove from the pan and keep warm in the oven. Peel and chop the shallots and add them to the pan. Sauté about 3 minutes on medium heat. Add the Madeira and mushrooms and boil for about 5 minutes, till very little Madeira remains. While it cooks, use a wooden spoon to scrape up the brown bits on the bottom of the pan. Add the whipping cream and thyme and boil until the liquid is reduced to the consistency of a sauce. This will take about 5 minutes. Pour the mushrooms and sauce over the pork and serve.

Makes 4 servings

Kitchen Table: California Chardonnay
Dinner Party: A better California Chardonnay

Gourmet Tourtière
Elizabeth Baird

Baird adapted this from a collection of Canadian recipes assembled by military wives at NATO headquarters in Belgium. This is a delicious chunky chicken and pork version that is perfect for cold-weather cooking. Thanks go to its originator, Carole Allaire.

Filling:

3	boneless skinless chicken breasts	3
1½ lb	lean boneless pork butt	750 g
2 tbsp	butter	25 mL
2	large onions, chopped	2
5 cups	sliced mushrooms	1.25 L
1 tsp	salt	5 mL
¼ tsp	pepper	1 mL
¼ tsp	ground cloves	1 mL
Pinch	dried thyme	Pinch
2 tbsp	vegetable oil	25 mL
¼ cup	all-purpose flour	50 mL
1 cup	dry white wine	250 mL
	Pastry for deep 9-inch (23 cm) double-crust pie	
1	egg yolk	1
1 tbsp	water	15 mL

Filling: Cut chicken and pork into ¼-inch (5 mm) cubes; set aside. In large skillet, melt butter over medium heat; cook onions for 5 minutes or until softened. Add mushrooms, salt, pepper, cloves, and thyme; increase heat to high and cook, stirring, for 5 to 7 minutes or until moisture evaporates. Transfer to bowl. Add half of the oil to skillet; brown chicken for 2 minutes and add to onion mixture. Toss pork with flour; brown in batches in remaining oil for 2 minutes. Return all pork to skillet; add wine and simmer, covered, for 10 to 15 minutes or until tender. Add to onion mixture. Taste and adjust seasoning; let cool.

On lightly floured surface, roll out half of the pastry; fit into deep 9-inch (23 cm) pie plate. Spoon filling into shell. Roll out remaining pastry. Whisk together egg yolk and water; brush some onto rim of pastry. Top filling with pastry; trim and flute edges. Brush with yolk mixture; slash steam vents. Bake at 450°F (230°C) for 10 minutes; reduce heat to 375°F (190°C) and bake for 40 to 45 minutes or until golden brown.

Makes 6 servings

Kitchen Table: Pinot Grigio
Dinner Party: Alsace Tokay Pinot Gris

Ribs Oriental Style
Rose Murray

Always a favourite, these are no-fuss ribs. Just start them marinating early in the morning or even the night before. Add fluffy steamed rice and a colourful stir-fried vegetable platter for a complete and satisfying supper.

4 lb	lean pork spareribs	2 kg
½ cup	hoisin sauce*	125 mL
2 tbsp	rice vinegar*	25 mL
1 tbsp	brown sugar	15 mL
1 tbsp	oyster sauce*	15 mL
½ tsp	five-spice powder*	2 mL
1	clove garlic, minced	1

Cut spareribs into serving pieces and place in single layer in shallow glass dish. In small bowl, stir together hoisin sauce, rice vinegar, sugar, oyster sauce, five-spice powder, and garlic. Pour over ribs, cover and refrigerate at least 4 hours or up to 24 hours, turning occasionally. Transfer ribs with any marinade to shallow foil-lined baking pan and roast, uncovered, in 400°F (200°C) oven for 10 minutes. Reduce heat to 350°F (180°C) and continue roasting a further 1 hour and 10 to 15 minutes or until tender, turning and basting occasionally.

  *Hoisin sauce and rice vinegar are available in most supermarkets. Look for oyster sauce and five-spice powder in oriental markets if not found in your supermarket.

Makes 4 to 6 servings

Kitchen Table: Australian Shiraz
Dinner Party: Red Zinfandel

Pork Chops with Clams
Dinah Koo

Portuguese in spirit, this hearty dish is an inspired combination of shellfish and meat. Terrific teamed with simple fried potatoes or rice, and watercress, says Koo.

4	pork chops OR pork steaks, (1-inch/2.5 cm) thick	4
1 tbsp	flour	15 mL
1 tbsp	olive oil	15 mL
1 cup	sliced onions	250 mL
Pinch	salt	Pinch
½ tsp	pepper	2 mL
8	cloves garlic, crushed	8
½ cup	white wine	125 mL
2 lb	fresh clams, well cleaned	1 kg
4 tbsp	chopped fresh parsley OR green onions	60 mL

Dredge pork chops with flour and set aside. In large frying pan with a lid, heat oil over high heat. Add pork chops and brown on both sides. Add onions and fry for 2 minutes. Add salt, pepper, garlic, and wine. Take care not to add too much salt — clams have a natural saltiness. Reduce heat to low, cover and simmer until tender, about 45 minutes. In the last 10 to 15 minutes of cooking, add the clams, cover and cook until clams open. Remove to serving dish and sprinkle liberally with chopped parsley or chopped green onions.

Makes 4 servings

*D**inah Koo is the owner of Dinah's Cupboard in Toronto, a gourmet food store and catering company.*

Kitchen Table: Macon Blanc
Dinner Party: Rheingau Riesling; Kabinett Trocken

VEGETABLES

The freshest vegetables — a perfect summer tomato, a shiny purple eggplant, crisp green beans — are beautiful sights to behold. They are also nutritious and low in fat. Vegetable dishes are an exciting accompaniment or can become a full, mouth-watering meal in themselves.

David's Black Bean Cabbage
Joanne Kates

Cabbage is being rediscovered. Good thing, too. This version, with its Oriental twist, is also terrific when tossed with diced cooked chicken or lamb. The black beans are available in Oriental food stores.

½	head green cabbage	½
2 tbsp	vegetable oil	25 mL
3	cloves garlic	3
1 tbsp	salted black beans	15 mL

Shred the cabbage. Heat the oil in a large, heavy-bottomed frying pan on high heat and fry the cabbage till very well browned, stirring often. This takes about 15 minutes. Dice the garlic and add to the browned cabbage. Fry for 2 minutes. Add the black beans and reduce heat to low. Cover the pan and cook 20 to 30 minutes.

Makes 3 servings

French Potato Cake
Kathleen Sloan

We found this wonderful side dish goes well with chicken. And we also loved it on its own for lunch!

3 lb	peeled red potatoes	1½ kg
¼ cup plus 2 tbsp	butter	50 mL plus 25 mL
3	large onions, thinly sliced	3
1 cup	grated Emmental	250 mL
	OR Gruyère cheese	
¼ tsp	salt	1 mL
	Freshly ground black pepper	
3 tbsp	unsalted butter	45 mL

Place potatoes in large saucepan and cover with cold water. Bring to a boil and cook over moderate heat around 25 to 30 minutes, then drain. Set aside to cool, then mash roughly with a fork. Heat ¼ cup butter in heavy, ovenproof skillet over medium heat. Add onions and sauté until soft and lightly browned, then add to the potatoes. Add cheese, salt, and pepper and blend well. In the same skillet, melt the 2 tbsp of butter, add the potoato mixture, and press down tightly with a spatula. Cover the pan and cook over moderate heat until the bottom of the cake is browned. Turn on broiler. When it is hot, place pan in oven about 5 or 6 inches beneath the broiler and broil until crisp and brown. Remove from oven and let stand for 10 minutes before serving.

Makes 6 servings

Oven Roasted Potatoes
Alice Krueger

We're always looking for new ways with potatoes, and this way is special, indeed. The balsamic vinegar is a brilliant touch.

4	medium red potatoes, scrubbed and cut in half	4
1	medium onion, chopped fine	1
2 tbsp	butter, melted	25 mL
3 tbsp	balsamic vinegar	45 mL
	Salt and pepper to taste	
6	sprigs fresh lemon thyme	6

Heat oven to 350°F (180°C). Place potatoes cut side down in a baking dish just big enough to hold them. Sprinkle chopped onion over top. Pour melted butter and vinegar over potatoes; season with salt and pepper. Tuck sprigs of lemon thyme around potatoes. Cover dish with aluminum foil and bake for 2 hours, turning potatoes over during last half hour to coat with butter and vinegar. Potatoes and bits of onion will be a deep golden brown.

Makes 4 servings

Alice Krueger is food editor for the Winnipeg Free Press.

Potato Pie
Susan Mendelson

Mashed potatoes are loved by young and old, and this dressed up version won't disappoint.

2 cups	mashed potatoes	500 mL
2 cups	cottage cheese	500 mL
½ cup	sour cream	125 mL
2	eggs, beaten	2
½ cup	grated onion	125 mL
Pinch	cayenne	Pinch
2 tsp	salt	10 mL
1	9-inch (23 cm) pie crust	1
¼ cup	grated Parmesan cheese	50 mL

Combine mashed potatoes, cottage cheese, sour cream, eggs, onion, cayenne, and salt. Put in pie crust. Sprinkle with grated Parmesan cheese. Bake at 425°F (220°C) for 50 minutes.

Makes 4 servings

Sautéed Rappini and Fennel
Joanne Kates

Now that these veggies are more widely available they can be enjoyed more often. Serve this as an accompaniment to veal. Or toss it with your favourite cooked pasta. Rappini is available in Italian food stores.

1	fennel bulb	1
½ lb	rappini	250 g
2	onions	2
3	cloves garlic	3
2 tbsp	olive oil	25 mL
2 tbsp	lemon juice	25 mL
⅓ cup	finely chopped Italian parsley	75 mL
	Salt and pepper to taste	

Cut off the fennel stems, cut the bulb in half, and core it. Slice thinly. Cut off and discard the tough bottom 2 inches (5 cm) of the rappini stems. Coarsely chop the rest. Wash the pieces and leave the water clinging to the leaves. Peel and slice the onions. Peel and dice the garlic.

  Heat the oil in a large, heavy-bottomed frying pan on medium-low heat and add the fennel, rappini, onions, and garlic. Cover the pan and cook 25 minutes, stirring occasionally. Add the lemon juice, parsley, salt, and pepper, and stir.

Makes 4 servings

Spinach with Nuts
Eileen Dwillies

Dwillies likes to serve this with sole — but we found it also delicious with lamb. With poached eggs on top, you can even enjoy this as a luncheon dish.

2 tbsp	butter	25 mL
¼ cup	nuts, such as walnuts, pine nuts, pecans, almonds	50 mL
1	bunch fresh spinach, washed and shaken dry	1
	Salt	
	Pepper	
	Nutmeg	

In a medium skillet, melt the butter. Sauté the nuts for 2 to 3 minutes, stirring occasionally. Remove the nuts and reserve. To the butter, add the slightly damp spinach leaves. Toss to heat through, about 4 minutes. Return the nuts to the pan. Add salt, pepper, and nutmeg to taste. Serve immediately.

Makes 2 servings

Spaghetti Squash
with a Great Deal of Cheese
Elizabeth Baird

Spaghetti squash is an amazing vegetable, and even people who aren't fussy about squash seem to like it. Baird taught us that, with cheese and butter, its long green strands are even better than fresh pasta.

1	spaghetti squash, about 3 lb (1.5 kg)	1
3 tbsp	butter	45 mL
⅓ cup	finely chopped onion OR shallots	75 mL
2 cups	grated Gruyère cheese, about 6 ounces (175 g)	500 mL
¾ tsp	salt	3 mL
¼ tsp	freshly ground pepper	1 mL
Pinch	freshly grated nutmeg	Pinch
½ cup	freshly grated Parmesan cheese	125 mL

Using an ice pick or skewer, prick to the centre of the squash in about 12 places. Set on a baking sheet and bake at 350°F (180°C) for 1½ hours, turning the squash over halfway through cooking time. Cut off top third of squash lengthwise, and spoon out the seeds and any liquid. Using a fork, scrape out the spaghetti-like strands from both pieces of squash and set to drain in a sieve for 10 minutes. Discard top shell.

In a small skillet, melt butter and sauté onion until translucent, about 4 minutes. Transfer to a bowl and stir in the squash, Gruyère, salt, pepper, and nutmeg. Taste and add more seasoning if necessary. Spoon into the bottom of the squash shell, sprinkle with Parmesan, and set on the baking sheet. Bake at 350°F (180°C) for 25 to 30 minutes, or until heated through and bubbly.

Makes 6 servings

Ratatouille Casserole
Monda Rosenberg

*M*onda

Rosenberg is food editor

of Chatelaine *magazine.*

Rosenberg reminded us about one of the all-time greats — this succulent vegetable casserole that is as good hot as it is at room temperature or cold.

¼ cup	olive oil OR butter	50 mL
2	cloves garlic, crushed	2
2	onions, finely chopped	2
1	medium-size eggplant, peeled and cut into ½ inch (1 cm) pieces	1
1	can tomatoes (28-ounce/796 mL), including juice	1
2 tbsp	capers, drained	25 mL
2 tsp	granulated sugar	10 mL
1 tsp	dried basil	5 mL
½ tsp	leaf oregano	2 mL
½ tsp	salt	2 mL
1	green pepper, seeded and cut into thin strips	1
1	zucchini, thinly sliced	1
2	containers cottage cheese (1 lb/500 g), well drained	2
6	eggs	6
½ cup	all-purpose flour	125 mL
3 cups	grated mozzarella cheese	750 mL

Heat oil in a large saucepan. Add garlic, onions, and eggplant and cook, stirring often, for 5 minutes. Add tomatoes and their juice, capers, sugar, basil, oregano, and salt. Break up tomatoes with a fork. Boil vigorously, uncovered, for 15 minutes to reduce liquid, stirring often. Add green pepper and zucchini and continue cooking for 5 minutes or until almost all liquid has evaporated. Stir often.

Meanwhile, heat oven to 350°F (180°C). Whirl cottage cheese with eggs, flour, and 1 cup grated mozzarella in a food processor or blender until fairly smooth. Evenly spread on bottom of a 9 by 13-inch (3.5 L) baking dish. Spoon vegetable mixture over top and cover with remaining 2 cups cheese. Casserole can be covered and refrigerated at this point, but is best prepared no more than 4 hours ahead. Bring to room temperature before baking.

Bake, uncovered, in the centre of the oven for 40 to 45 minutes, or until browned. Let stand for at least 5 minutes before cutting. This casserole does not freeze well.

Makes 12 servings

Garden Stir Fry
Dinah Koo

Everyone loves a colourful, crisp stir fry, and this one is a basic recipe that's the best. Use any vegetable that's in season. And serve it with anything your heart desires.

1 lb	parsnips, sliced diagonally into ¼ inch (6 mm) pieces	500 g
1 lb	green beans, cut into 1½ inch (4 cm) pieces	500 g
1 lb	yellow beans, cut into 1½ inch (4 cm) pieces	500 g
1	medium-sized cauliflower, cut into small florets	1
2	bunches broccoli, cut into small florets	2
2	bunches medium-sized carrots, sliced diagonally into ¼ inch (6 mm) pieces	2
½ to 1 cup	butter and olive oil for cooking	125 to 250 mL
1	large red onion, cut into ¼ inch (6 mm) wedges	1
2	zucchini, sliced into ¼ inch (6 mm) pieces	2
⅓ cup	soy sauce	75 mL
	Salt	
	Pepper	
4	cloves garlic, minced	4
2	red bell peppers, cut into ¼ inch (6 mm) strips	2
1 lb	snow or sugar snap peas, strings removed	500 g
¼ cup	lemon juice (optional)	50 mL

Bring a large pot of salted water to a boil. Blanch parsnips for several minutes, until slightly softened but still crisp. Drain and run under cold water to stop the cooking. Repeat blanching with beans, then cauliflower, then broccoli, then carrots. This can be done a few hours ahead of serving time.

Have ready a large casserole or foil roasting pan large enough to hold the vegetables. Half an hour before serving, heat oven to 300°F (150°C). Then heat enough olive oil over medium-high heat to coat the bottom of a large frying pan. Add a little butter. Sauté onion for a minute, then add zucchini and stir for another minute. Sprinkle on a little soy sauce, salt, pepper, and a little garlic. Transfer to large casserole or roasting pan and keep hot in oven.

To the frying pan add more oil, butter, garlic, and as much of the blanched vegetables as can be tossed and sautéed at one time. Sauté quickly for 2 to 3 minutes, sprinkling with a little soy sauce, salt, and pepper. Transfer to large pan in oven. Repeat until all blanched vegetables have been sautéed. Peppers and snow peas should be cooked last; they require only 1 to 2 minutes. Combine everything in the large pan. Season to taste and sprinkle with lemon juice, if desired.

Makes 20 servings

Three-Layered Vegetable Terrine
Rose Reisman

This delicious and beautiful terrine is almost all you need to accompany a special roast of beef or grilled veal chops.

1 lb	carrots	500 g
1 lb	cauliflower	500 g
1 lb	broccoli	500 g
3	egg yolks	3
3	eggs	3
6 tbsp	butter	90 mL
	Salt	
	Pepper	
	Fresh parsley to garnish	

Heat oven to 350°F (180°C). Line a loaf pan with buttered parchment paper. Cut each vegetable into pieces, keeping each separate. Cook in boiling water just until barely done. Strain, still keeping separate. Place the carrots in a food processor, then add 1 egg yolk, 1 egg, 2 tbsp (25 mL) butter, salt, and pepper. Process until smooth. Pour into loaf pan. Repeat for cauliflower, then for broccoli. Cover loaf pan with parchment paper. Place in a bain-marie (water bath) and bake for 1 hour. Cool for approximately 30 minutes, then invert. Cut into slices.

Makes 8 servings

Another combination of vegetables can be substituted. Use different coloured vegetables.

Roasted Fall Vegetables
Rose Murray

We took Murray's advice and tried this dish when markets were overflowing with myriad colourful vegetables. It's perfect to pop into the oven alongside a chicken or capon.

8	small potatoes, scrubbed and quartered	8
2	onions, cut into wedges	2
4	cloves garlic, crushed	4
¼ cup	olive oil	50 mL
¼ tsp	dried thyme	1 mL
¼ tsp	dried rosemary	1 mL
1	medium butternut squash, peeled and cut into ¾ inch (2 cm) cubes	1
1	red pepper, cut into ¾ inch (2 cm) chunks	1
	Chopped fresh parsley	

In roasting pan, toss potatoes, onions, and garlic with 3 tbsp (45 mL) of the oil. Sprinkle with thyme and rosemary; roast, uncovered, at 375°F (190°C) for 35 minutes, gently turning once with a metal spatula. Toss squash and red pepper with remaining oil; add to pan and continue roasting for 10 to 20 minutes longer, or until all vegetables are tender. Sprinkle with parsley.

Makes 6 servings

PASTA

As a starter, a side dish, or a sophisticated meal, pasta is a most versatile and popular staple. High in carbohydrates and low in fat, it is also exceptionally nutritious.

Fettucine with Artichokes
Umberto Menghi

This meatless pasta meal for artichoke lovers can be made in a flash with ingredients that are on hand or are easy to find.

¾ lb	fettucine	375 g
¼ cup	butter	50 mL
2	cloves garlic, crushed	2
1	can artichoke hearts (14 oz/398 g), drained and quartered	1
¼ cup	white wine	50 mL
1¼ cups	whipping cream	300 mL
	Salt and pepper to taste	
½ cup	Parmesan cheese	125 mL

Cook fettucine in boiling water until al dente (firm to the bite). Drain and set aside. Meanwhile, prepare sauce. Heat butter in large skillet; add garlic and sauté until light brown. Add artichoke hearts and wine and simmer for 2 minutes. Add cream and cook over medium heat until cream begins to bubble, approximately 3 minutes. Add salt, pepper, and pasta to sauce, and toss. Add Parmesan cheese and toss until cheese has melted.

Makes 4 to 6 servings

Umberto Menghi is one of Vancouver's leading restaurateurs and author of numerous cookbooks.

Substitute table cream or half and half for heavy cream if fat and calories are a concern.

Kitchen Table: Chilean Sauvignon Blanc
Dinner Party: Pouilly-Fumé

Pasta Shells Stuffed with Cheese in a Creamy Tomato Sauce
Umberto Menghi

With its mild cheese filling, this traditional Italian dish is welcome either at a fancy dinner party or as a comfort food.

½ lb	jumbo pasta shells OR 12 manicotti shells	500 g
1 cup	ricotta cheese	250 mL
½ cup	Parmesan cheese	125 mL
¼ cup	grated soft, mild cheese (Havarti, brick, etc.)	50 mL
¼ cup	finely chopped chives OR green onions	50 mL
2	egg yolks	2
1 tbsp	butter	15 mL
¼ cup	whipping cream	50 mL
2 cups	prepared tomato sauce	500 mL
⅓ cup	Parmesan cheese Chives for garnish	75 mL

Cook shells in boiling water until al dente (firm to the bite). Drain and set aside. Meanwhile, prepare sauce. Combine the cheeses, the chives, and the egg yolks. Stuff pasta shells with the mixture. Butter the bottom of a large baking dish and pour in the cream. Place stuffed pasta shells in dish; pour the tomato sauce over the shells. Sprinkle with Parmesan cheese. Cover and bake at 375°F (160°C) for approximately 20 minutes. Garnish with chopped chives.

Makes 4 to 5 servings

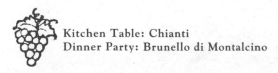

Kitchen Table: Chianti
Dinner Party: Brunello di Montalcino

Linguine with Spicy Sausage
Umberto Menghi

Everybody loves this simple thin pasta coated with morsels of spicy sausage. It's got zing!

¾ lb	linguine	375 g
¾ lb	sausage, medium to spicy	375 g
¼ cup	olive oil	50 mL
	Hot red chili pepper, dry or fresh, to taste	
12	chopped basil leaves OR 2 tsp (10 mL) dry	12
	Salt and pepper to taste	
¼ to ⅓ cup	Parmesan cheese	50 to 75 mL
1 tbsp	chopped parsley	15 mL

Cook linguine in boiling water until al dente (firm to the bite). Drain and set aside. Meanwhile, prepare sauce. Remove skin from sausage, chop, and add with oil to large skillet. Sauté until sausage is nearly done, approximately 5 minutes. Add chili pepper, basil, salt, and pepper and simmer for 2 minutes. Add pasta to skillet and toss. If pasta appears dry, add a little more oil. Sprinkle with Parmesan cheese and parsley and serve.

Makes 4 servings

Kitchen Table: Côtes du Rhône (red)
Dinner Party: Zinfandel (red)

Penne with Italian Sausage, Tomato, and Herbs

Anne Lindsay

This favourite family dish, from Lighthearted Everyday Cooking, *has taken over from spaghetti in Lindsay's home. Spice it up with Macedonian or spicy Italian sausages, or make it less spicy by using sweet Italian sausages. Or try substituting shrimp for the sausage — or use half and half!*

1 lb	hot Italian sausage	500 g
1 lb	penne OR corkscrew-shaped pasta	500 g
1 tsp	vegetable oil	5 mL
1	large onion, chopped	1
3	cloves garlic, minced	3
1	can tomatoes (28 oz/796 mL)	1
	undrained, coarsely chopped	1
2 tsp	dried basil	10 mL
1 tsp	dried oregano	5 mL
½ cup	chopped fresh parsley	125 mL
	Freshly ground pepper	
2 tbsp	freshly grated Parmesan	25 mL
	cheese (optional)	

In skillet, cook sausage over medium heat until no longer pink in centre, about 15 to 20 minutes; drain well, then cut into thin round slices. Meanwhile, in large pot of boiling water, cook pasta until tender yet firm; drain and return to pot. In nonstick pan, heat oil over medium heat; add onion and cook until tender, about 5 minutes. Add garlic, tomatoes, basil, and oregano; simmer, uncovered, for 10 minutes; add cooked sausage. Pour sauce over pasta and toss to mix. Sprinkle with parsley and pepper to taste; add Parmesan and toss again.

For pasta with shrimp and tomatoes: Substitute 1 lb (500 g) large cooked shrimp; or use ½ lb (250 g) each of cooked shrimp and sausage. Add shrimp to tomato mixture when adding cooked sausage.

Makes 6 servings

Kitchen Table: Barbera
Dinner Party: Barbaresco

Pasta with Shrimp, Zucchini, and Mushrooms
Anne Lindsay

This is perfect for entertaining and is also a good summer pasta dish. From Lighthearted Everyday Cooking, this dish lends itself to a variety of fresh herbs — throw in basil or dill. And while we recommend penne or rigatoni, you can experiment using other pasta shapes, too.

1 lb	pasta (penne OR rigatoni)	500 g
3 tbsp	olive oil	45 mL
4	small (7-inch/18 cm) zucchini, julienned	4
½ lb	mushrooms, sliced	250 g
2 lb	large raw shrimp, peeled and deveined	1 kg
3	cloves garlic, minced	3
1	large tomato, diced	1
½ cup	chopped fresh parsley	125 mL
¼ cup	freshly grated Parmesan cheese	50 mL
2 tbsp	fresh lemon juice	25 mL
	Salt and pepper	

In large pot of boiling water, cook pasta until tender but firm; drain and return to pot. Meanwhile, in a large, nonstick skillet, heat 1 tbsp (15 mL) of the oil over high heat; add zucchini and mushrooms and stir-fry until tender-crisp, about 3 minutes. Transfer to bowl. In the same skillet, heat remaining oil over high heat, then add shrimp and garlic; cook, stirring, for 3 minutes or until shrimp is opaque. Add tomato and cook for 1 minute. Add shrimp and zucchini mixtures (including all liquids) to pot with hot pasta. Add parsley, cheese, and lemon juice; toss to mix. Season with salt and pepper.

Makes 8 servings

Kitchen Table: Dry Orvieto
Dinner Party: Alsace Riesling

Pasta with Fresh Tomatoes, Basil, and Parmesan

Alison Fryer

Alison Fryer is the manager of The Cookbook Store in Toronto.

Sometimes simple is absolutely best. And simple is always best when you use fresh tomatoes and basil and freshly grated cheese and ground pepper.

1 lb	pasta	500 g
1 cup	freshly grated Parmesan reggiano (and more for serving)	250 mL
	Freshly ground black pepper	
6	fresh tomatoes, peeled, cut into eighths, and lightly salted	6
	Fresh basil torn into small pieces	

Cook pasta until al dente, approximately 10 minutes. Toss with cheese and pepper. Place in individual bowls and garnish with tomatoes and basil. Top with extra Parmesan.

Variations: Stir-fry 3 cups of seasonal vegetables — for example zucchini, carrots, and broccoli — in olive oil, then toss with pasta.

Makes 4 servings

Kitchen Table: Beaujolais
Dinner Party: Chianti Classico Riserva

Tomato, Bocconcini, and Basil in a Balsamic Vinaigrette
Vicki Newbury

You can't beat this fabulous pasta that's a twist on the salad of the same name.

1 ¼ lb	pasta	625 g
¾ cup	olive oil	175 mL
1 tbsp	red wine vinegar	15 mL
¼ cup	balsamic vinegar	50 mL
4	cloves garlic, chopped	4
4	fresh tomatoes, cut in wedges	4
1 ¼ cups	loosely packed basil, coarsely chopped	300 mL
½ lb	Bocconcini cheese, sliced	250 g
	Salt	
	Freshly ground pepper	

Vicki Newbury is head chef at Chez Piggy restaurant in Kingston, Ontario and co-author of The Chez Piggy Cookbook.

Cook the pasta until al dente, about 10 minutes. Drain. In a heavy frying pan, over low heat, warm the oil, vinegars, and garlic. Toss in the tomatoes, basil, Bocconcini, and hot pasta. Season with salt and pepper. Serve warm as the cheese begins to melt.

Makes 6 servings as a main course

Classic Pesto Sauce
Noël Richardson

Summer is the best time to turn that backyard basil crop into something to zip up soups and pastas all winter long.

2 cups	freshly washed, firmly packed basil leaves	500 mL
2 to 4	cloves garlic, peeled and crushed	2 to 4
½ cup	olive OR vegetable oil	125 mL
3 tbsp	pine nuts	45 mL
1 cup	freshly grated Parmesan cheese	250 mL

Put basil and garlic in a blender or food processor. Pour in oil and process until smooth. Add pine nuts and process for a few seconds. Stir in Parmesan cheese. If sauce is too thick, add more oil or a few spoonfuls of pasta or vegetable cooking water.

If you are not using the pesto sauce right away, put in a jar in the refrigerator with a skin of oil on top and cover with plastic wrap. Pesto sauce will keep like this for several weeks.

To freeze pesto sauce for the winter, process basil, garlic, and oil and freeze in plastic cartons. To use, thaw slowly at room temperature, then add pine nuts and Parmesan cheese before serving.

Do not heat pesto, as it turns very dark and is unappetizing.

Serve pesto sauce with 1 lb (500 g) pasta. Cook pasta al dente. Pasta and pesto sauce can be tossed together in a large bowl or each person can put sauce on his or her own pasta. Sprinkle with extra freshly grated Parmesan cheese.

Makes 4 servings

 If basil leaves are unavailable substitute parsley leaves or spinach leaves. A combination with basil is excellent.

Sun-Dried Tomato Pesto
Rose Reisman

Now that sun-dried tomatoes are readily available, you can make this fine sauce as an alternative to the traditional basil-based pesto. If you buy the sun-dried tomatoes in a package or in bulk, blanch in boiling water for 2 minutes, then marinate in jars of olive oil. They keep almost forever in a cool, dry place.

3 cups	sun-dried tomatoes, drained and well-packed	750 mL
1¼ cups	olive oil	300 mL
¼ cup	oil from the sun-dried tomatoes	50 mL
1 cup	grated Parmesan cheese	250 mL
¾ cup	toasted pine nuts	175 mL
¾ cup	well-packed parsley leaves	175 mL
4	cloves garlic	4

Place all ingredients into a food processor. Grind until the sauce is fairly smooth. Toss with cooked pasta. Serve with toasted pine nuts and 4 oz (125 g) grated Asiago cheese.

Makes 4 to 6 servings

Linguini Picante All'Aglio e Olivi
Ladka Sweeney

Olive lovers adore this. So does anyone who loves food with a distinct Mediterranean flavour. Best of all, it's on the table in less than 30 minutes, so you can easily serve it at a mid-week dinner party.

1 lb	linguini, fresh OR dry	500 g
3 tbsp	olive oil with hot pepper essence	45 mL
20	ripe oil-cured olives, pips removed, coarsely cut	20
8	cloves garlic, peeled, flattened with knife	8
2 tbsp	chopped hot red pepper	25 mL
7 oz	sliced mushrooms, the "wilder" the better	200 g
3	sprigs fresh cilantro	3
	Crusty bread	

Cook pasta until al dente. In a large pan, heat oil. Add olives, garlic, hot pepper, and mushrooms. Cook over low heat for 10 minutes, stirring constantly. Toss with the hot cooked pasta. Garnish with cilantro and serve with crusty bread.

Makes 4 servings

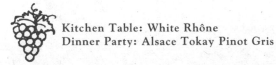

Kitchen Table: White Rhône
Dinner Party: Alsace Tokay Pinot Gris

Michelle's Killer Linguini
Michelle Ramsay

If you want your pasta to stand up and sing, this dish with its melted cheese, tangy garlic, and red-hot pepper is just the ticket.

8 oz	Brie cheese	225 g
¾ lb	dried linguini	375 g
⅔ cup	extra virgin olive oil	75 mL
3 to 4	large cloves garlic, minced	3 to 4
2	large shallots, minced	2
1	habanero (Scotch bonnet) pepper, fresh OR bottled, cut in half	1
4	red bell peppers, peeled, seeded, and cut into ½-inch (1 cm) wide strips	4
8 oz	sliced fresh mushrooms	225 mL
½ cup	chopped fresh basil OR coriander	125 mL
	Salt and pepper to taste	
	Basil leaves	

Remove peel from Brie. This is best done when cheese is cold, using a wet knife. Cut peeled Brie into 1-inch (2.5 cm) chunks and set aside. Cook pasta, drain, and set aside. In a large skillet, heat olive oil and sauté garlic, shallots, and habanero pepper over medium-low until garlic is fragrant, about 1 minute. Don't let it burn. Add bell peppers and cook about 5 minutes. Add mushrooms and sauté another couple of minutes. Toss cooked pasta with sautéed vegetable mixture; add Brie and toss again. Add chopped basil or coriander and mix well. Season with salt and pepper and chili peppers, if you are brave. Garnish with additional basil or coriander leaves.

Makes 4 servings

Kitchen Table: Muscadet
Dinner Party: Vernaccia di San Gimigniano

Ravioli with Nutty Cream Sauce
Rose Reisman

This is a lovely departure from traditional tomato-based pasta, and a welcome first course to a special dinner.

¼ cup	hazelnuts	50 mL
2 tbsp	walnuts	25 mL
⅓ cup	pine nuts	75 mL
⅓ lb	ravioli OR tortellini	375 g
2 tbsp	butter	25 mL
¾ cup	whipping cream	175 mL
	Salt and pepper to taste	
¼ cup	Parmesan cheese	50 mL

Combine the nuts and finely chop. (Use the amounts shown or any combination you like.) Set aside. Cook pasta until al dente (firm to the bite), drain, and set aside. To prepare sauce, heat butter and cream in a saucepan. Add salt and pepper along with half the nut mixture and cook just until cream boils. Add pasta and toss. Sprinkle pasta with cheese and remaining nuts.

   Note: Toasting the hazelnuts will produce a more distinct flavour. Toast either on top of the stove or in the oven at 400°F (200°C) just until golden.

Makes 3 to 4 servings

Kitchen Table: Chilean Chardonnay
Dinner Party: Meursault

North Thai Spaghetti Sauce
Peter Cochrane

For some who like it hot, hot, hot, this tomato pasta sauce will be a welcome treat. Six chilies make a pleasant version.

1 lb	spaghetti	500 g
12	large, dried red Thai chilies, or more to taste	12
6	cloves garlic, peeled	6
1 tsp	salt	5 mL
2 tbsp	vegetable oil	25 mL
1 ½ lbs	lean pork, ground finely	750 g
4	ripe, fresh tomatoes, peeled and chopped	4
4	green onions, chopped	4
2 tbsp	nam pla (Thai fish sauce)	25 mL
	Fresh coriander leaves, chopped	
	Cucumber, peeled and finely diced	
	Beans, snapped into short lengths	
	Carrots, sliced thinly	
	Celery, sliced thin	

Peter Cochrane has been watching and reporting on the Ottawa food scene for more than 20 years. He appears on CBC Radio and CJOH television and teaches cooking on the side.

Soak the chilies in hot water for about 15 minutes and then reduce them to a paste by pounding them in a mortar with the garlic and salt. You can use a blender if you wish, but a mortar and pestle do a better job. Heat the oil in a heavy saucepan and sauté the chili-garlic mixture for about 5 minutes, making sure that it does not stick to the pan. Add the pork, sauté it until it is well browned and then add the tomatoes. Add the chopped green onions and the nam pla and cook the mixture for about half an hour uncovered, stirring when necessary to make sure that it does not stick. Cook pasta to your taste and place it in a serving bowl. Spoon the sauce over it and serve it garnished with the coriander leaves and the fresh vegetables.

Makes 4 servings

Handle the chilies with care — wash hands after use.

Spaghettini with Asparagus and Morels
Kathleen Walker

After brief stints in other journalistic areas, Kathleen Walker took to the job of Food Writer/Editor at the Ottawa Citizen like a hand to an oven mitt. Can you imagine a better job than culling through gorgeous cookbooks, tasting, retesting and adapting recipes, eating the results and getting paid for it?

This is a lovely marriage of morels and spring asparagus, and a nice change from tomato-based pasta for dinner or brunch.

15 to 20	morels	15 to 20
1 tbsp	unsalted butter	15 mL
3	large shallots, finely chopped	3
½ cup	white wine	125 mL
1 cup	homemade chicken stock OR canned chicken broth (½ cup/125 mL) and water (⅓ cup/125 mL) Salt and freshly ground black pepper, to taste	250 mL
1 cup	whipping cream Grating of nutmeg	250 mL
1 lb	thin asparagus, trimmed and cut diagonally into 1-inch (2.5 cm) lengths	500 g
1 lb	spaghettini	500 g

Halve the morels, wash thoroughly, and drain. Set aside. In saucepan over medium-low heat, melt the butter and add the shallots. Sauté, stirring, until shallots are translucent and tender. Add the wine and bring to a boil. Add the stock, morels, salt, and pepper, and simmer until the liquid has reduced to ¾ cup (175 mL). Add the cream, bring to a boil, and let simmer gently, stirring occasionally, until the sauce thickens enough to coat a wooden spoon — about 15 to 20 minutes. Add a grating of nutmeg. (The sauce can be made a day in advance to this point and refrigerated; reheat on medium-high in the microwave.) Cook the asparagus in boiling salted water for about 2 to 3 minutes (depending on thickness), until just tender. Drain and run under cold water.

To assemble: Cook the pasta in a large pot of boiling salted water. Drain and put pasta in large, warm bowl. Meanwhile, add the asparagus to the sauce and reheat gently. Toss gently with the pasta.

Makes 6 servings as an appetizer, 4 as a main course

Spicy Thai Noodles
Marion Kane

Thai cooking is hot, and this dish is delish. All the Oriental ingredients including the rice sticks (also called rice vermicelli) can be found at almost any Chinese grocery store.

½ lb	dried rice noodles	250 g
¼ cup	vegetable oil	50 mL
3	cloves garlic, minced	3
½ lb	skinless, boneless chicken breast, diced	250 g
½ lb	shrimp, peeled, deveined, diced	250 g
2	eggs, beaten	2
2 cups	bean sprouts	500 mL
⅓ cup	unsalted peanuts, coarsely ground	75 mL
½ cup	ketchup	50 mL
3 tbsp	Oriental fish sauce	45 mL
2 tbsp	lemon OR lime juice	25 mL
2 tsp	soy sauce	10 mL
1 tsp	Oriental chili sauce OR chili paste	5 mL
1 tsp	granulated sugar	5 mL
3	green onions, thinly sliced	3

Place noodles in large bowl and cover with hot water. Let stand 20 minutes or until softened. Drain well. Heat oil in a large skillet or wok over medium-high heat. Add garlic, chicken, and shrimp and stir-fry about 1½ minutes or until chicken is nearly cooked through. Add egg; let set slightly, then stir to scramble. Add drained noodles; then add bean sprouts and peanuts and stir-fry until heated through, about 4 minutes. In a small bowl, combine ketchup, fish sauce, lemon juice, soy sauce, chili sauce, and sugar. Add to wok; stir-fry until noodles are well coated. Garnish with onion.

Makes 4 servings

Kitchen Table: Alsace Gewürztraminer
Dinner Party: German Riesling Spätlese Trocken

RICE, GRAINS AND LEGUMES

In these health-conscious times, there is no better bet than a main course of beans, rice, or couscous. Not only are these earthy alternatives low in fat, high in fibre, and easy on the pocketbook, they also blend well with robust flavourings such as garlic, chili, and curry to make hearty meals.

Couscous with Chick Peas, Vegetables, and Raisins
Cynthia Wine

Now that more of us are interested in eating less meat, this recipe is a welcome addition. And it's one that still impresses dinner guests — especially if they've travelled to the North African countries of Morocco, Tunisia, or Algeria where couscous is the national dish. Note that the chick peas must be soaked overnight.

¼ cup	chick peas	50 mL
2 lb	boneless lamb, cubed	1 kg
1	onion, quartered	1
2	carrots, coarsely chopped	2
2 tbsp	olive oil	25 mL
2	bay leaves, coarsely chopped	2
¼ cup	tomato paste	50 mL
6 to 8 cups	water	1.5 to 2 L
2	small fresh hot red chilies, minced	2
2 tsp	ground cumin	10 mL
1 tsp	ground ginger	5 mL
½ tsp	cinnamon	2 mL
1 tsp	salt	5 mL
5	stalks celery, coarsely chopped	5
2	small turnips, peeled and cut into chunks	2
1	small sweet potato, peeled and quartered	1
2	green peppers, seeded and quartered	2
1	medium potato, peeled and quartered	1
¼ cup	raisins	50 mL
1 lb	packaged couscous	500 g
2 tbsp	butter (optional)	25 mL
	Harissa sauce (recipe follows)	

Soak the chick peas in water overnight. Drain, cover with fresh water, and cook for 1½ hours. Drain and set aside. In a large pot, sauté the lamb, onion, and carrots in the olive oil just until meat begins to brown. Add chick peas, bay leaves, tomato paste, and 3 cups (750 mL) of the water. Cover and simmer for 30 minutes. Then add chilies, cumin, ginger, cinnamon, salt, celery, turnip, sweet potato, green peppers, potato, and raisins. Pour in remaining water. Simmer for 30 minutes. Prepare couscous according to package directions. Arrange couscous on a large, warm platter. Toss with the butter, if using, and ladle some broth over the couscous. Arrange vegetables and meat over the couscous and serve with the rest of the broth and a bowl of Harissa sauce.

Makes 6 to 8 servings

Harissa Sauce:

6	dried hot red chilies	6
2 tbsp	caraway seeds	25 mL
2	cloves garlic	2
1 tbsp	coarse salt	15 mL
⅓ cup (approx)	vegetable oil	75 mL

Soak the chilies in cold water for 1 hour to soften them. Split the chilies and remove the stems and seeds. Pound the chilies in a mortar with the caraway seeds, garlic, and salt until they form a paste. Mix in enough oil to make the paste liquid. To use the sauce, dilute a bit in a spoonful of broth and pour over each serving of the couscous.

Makes about ½ cup (125 mL)

Curried Lentils with Coriander
Anne Lindsay

We go back to this yummy and authentic Indian dish again and again. Thanks to Hajaa Wilson, a volunteer for the Heart and Stroke Foundation of Ontario, who taught it to Lindsay.

2 cups	green lentils	500 mL
2 tbsp	vegetable oil	25 mL
2	medium onions, chopped	2
1 tsp	ginger	5 mL
1 tsp	coriander	5 mL
1 tsp	cumin	5 mL
1 tsp	turmeric	5 mL
1 tsp	minced garlic	5 mL
½ tsp	salt	2 mL
3	whole cloves	3
2	whole cardamom	2
1	3-inch (8 cm) stick cinnamon OR ½ tsp (2 mL) ground	1
¼ tsp	hot pepper flakes	1 mL
1 cup	chopped tomatoes, fresh OR canned	250 mL
⅓ cup	chopped green onion, including tops	75 mL
¼ cup	chopped fresh coriander	50 mL

Wash lentils in cold water; drain. In saucepan, combine 6 cups (1.5 L) water and lentils. Bring to a boil; reduce heat, cover, and simmer for 20 to 30 minutes, or until lentils are tender; drain. Meanwhile, in large saucepan over medium heat, combine oil, onion, ginger, coriander, cumin, turmeric, garlic, salt, cloves, cardamom, cinnamon, and hot pepper flakes; cook for 10 minutes or until onions are softened, stirring frequently. Add tomatoes and drained lentils; simmer over low heat for 3 minutes. Remove cloves, cardamom, and cinnamon stick and discard. Stir in green onion and fresh coriander. Serve hot.

Makes 8 servings

Nutty Brown Rice
Margo Oliver

*M*argo Oliver
was born in Winnipeg
and received her home
economics education at
the University of
Manitoba and the
University of Minnesota.
She was food editor of
the now-defunct
Weekend *magazine and
during her career has
written seven cookbooks.*

We agree with Oliver, who likes this tasty healthful dish because it can add a little glamour to an otherwise ordinary meal. This dish is delicious with poultry and can be prepared ahead, then baked when needed.

2 tbsp	butter OR margarine	25 mL
1 cup	chopped onion	250 mL
1 cup	chopped celery	250 mL
1	clove garlic, crushed	1
1 cup	uncooked brown rice	250 mL
2 ½ cups	chicken stock	625 mL
1 tsp	seasoned salt	5 mL
	Black pepper	
1 cup	chopped, lightly toasted pecans	250 mL

Heat oven to 350°F (180°C). Butter a 1 ½ quart (1.5 L) casserole. Melt butter or margarine in a large saucepan over medium heat. Add onion, celery, and garlic and cook, stirring, for 5 minutes. Add rice, chicken stock, seasoned salt, and pepper. Pour into prepared casserole, cover, and bake 1 hour. Uncover, add nuts, and stir lightly with a fork. Bake, uncovered, until liquid is absorbed but rice is still moist, about 15 minutes.

Makes six servings

Jamaican Rice and Peas
Carol Ferguson

Ferguson learned to make this in Jamaica many years ago, and now it's a family favourite with curried chicken or fish. With so many West Indian communities across Canada these days, finding the ingredients is easier than ever. These peas are sometimes called cow peas.

½ cup	small red dried peas	125 mL
1½ cups	boiling salted water	375 mL
½ cup	canned coconut milk	125 mL
1 cup	uncooked rice	250 mL
1	small onion, chopped	1
¼ tsp	dried thyme	1 mL
½ tsp	salt	2 mL
Pinch	black pepper	Pinch

In saucepan, boil peas in water until tender, about 1 hour. Drain, reserving cooking liquid. Measure liquid and add coconut milk plus enough water to make 2 cups (500 mL). Return liquid to peas in saucepan. Add rice, onion, thyme, salt, and pepper. Cover and simmer until liquid is absorbed and rice is tender, about 30 minutes. Add more salt and pepper if needed.

Makes about 4 servings

Carol Ferguson is a Toronto food writer, editor, and consultant. She was food editor of Canadian Living *magazine from 1975-87, editor of* Canadian Living's FOOD *magazines and is author of* The Canadian Living Cookbook *and* The Canadian Living Entertaining Cookbook.

Risotto with Pine Nuts and Spinach
Rose Reisman

Reisman gave us this risotto, in which the buttery rice is enhanced by the addition of cheese, spinach, and pine nuts. It's a meal in itself, or a special first course for a formal dinner.

¾ lb	chopped spinach, fresh OR frozen	375 g
⅓ cup	pine nuts	75 mL
2 tbsp	butter	25 mL
1 tbsp	oil	15 mL
2 tbsp	finely chopped onion	25 mL
1 cup	rice, preferably Arborio	250 mL
3 cups	chicken stock	750 mL
¼ cup	Parmesan cheese	50 mL

Cook spinach in boiling water until done. Squeeze out moisture. Set aside. Toast pine nuts in skillet, or bake at 400°F (200°C) until lightly browned. Set aside.

Heat butter and oil in medium pan. Add onion and cook until soft. Add rice and sauté for 2 minutes. Slowly add chicken stock and cook over medium heat, stirring often, until all liquid is absorbed, approximately 15 to 20 minutes. Add spinach and pine nuts. Remove from heat. Add Parmesan cheese and serve.

Makes 4 to 6 servings

Risotto with Sweet Sausage and Vegetables
Rose Reisman

We like this creamy risotto with the yummy addition of crisp bacon and sweet sausage. It's a trio that's tops in taste and texture.

1 tsp	olive oil	5 mL
¼ cup	butter	50 mL
1	small onion, chopped	1
1	small carrot, diced	1
1	celery stalk, diced	1
2 oz	bacon, preferably Italian pancetta, chopped	50 g
6 oz	sweet sausage	125 g
1 cup	rice, preferably Arborio	250 mL
3½ cups (approx)	beef broth	875 mL
¼ cup	Parmesan cheese	50 mL

Heat oil and butter in medium-sized skillet. Add onion, carrot, celery, and bacon and cook until vegetables become soft. Remove skin from sausage and chop. Add to skillet, cooking over medium heat until sausage is almost done. Use a fork to crumble sausage. Add rice and sauté until rice is light brown. Slowly add the beef broth, stirring often, and cook until all the liquid has been absorbed, about 20 to 25 minutes. Remove from heat. Add cheese and serve hot.

Makes 4 to 6 servings

Wild Rice and Mushroom Pilaf
Elizabeth Baird

*Baird's wild rice, mushrooms, and hazelnuts are an unforgettable combo.
Even though it has an elegant note to it, we like this recipe for family suppers.*

2 tbsp	butter	25 mL
2 cups	sliced mushrooms, about 6 oz (175 g)	500 mL
1	onion, chopped	1
1 cup	wild rice, rinsed	250 mL
1 ½ cups	chicken stock	375 mL
¼ cup	hazelnuts	50 mL
¼ cup	chopped fresh parsley	50 mL
2	green onions, chopped	2
	Salt	
	Pepper	

In large heavy saucepan, melt butter over medium-high heat; add
mushrooms and onion and cook, stirring often, for 5 minutes or until
tender. Add rice, stirring to coat grains. Stir in stock; cover and bring to
boil. Reduce heat to medium-low and simmer, partially covered, for 45 to
55 minutes, or until rice is tender and liquid is absorbed. While rice is
cooking, toast the hazelnuts. Spread them on a baking sheet and bake at
350°F (180°C) for 6 to 8 minutes, or until golden brown. Wrap in a clean
tea towel and rub off skins, then chop.

   When rice is done, stir in parsley, hazelnuts, green onions, and salt and
pepper to taste.

Makes 6 to 8 servings

Rice with Fresh Spring Vegetables
Rose Reisman

This is so yummy it's like comfort food — soothing, healthy, and delicious, even on its own.

2 cups	fresh spring vegetables (combination of zucchini, eggplant, eggplant, bell peppers, etc.)	500 mL
¼ cup	butter	175 mL
½ lb	rice	250 g
3 cups	chicken broth	750 mL
1 cup	tomato sauce	250 mL
	Salt and pepper to taste	
¼ cup	Parmesan cheese	50 mL

Cut up vegetables and cook for 1 minute in boiling water. Drain and set aside. Melt butter in medium-sized pan. Add rice and sauté until light brown, about 5 minutes.

Slowly add chicken broth to rice and stir often until all the liquid is absorbed, about 20 to 25 minutes. Add drained vegetables. Add salt, pepper, and Parmesan cheese, mix, and serve.

Makes 4 to 6 servings

Lemon Herb Rice
Gay Cook

ay Cook
is food writer for the
Ottawa Sun *and owns a*
company called Mrs.
Cooks Foods, which
produces heritage fruit
cakes and plum
puddings every
Christmas.

You can't beat this rice recipe that is so versatile it's good hot, at room temperature, or chilled. And it goes beautifully with fish, lamb, chicken, or beef!

1 tbsp	butter	15 mL
¼ cup	finely chopped onion	50 mL
1 cup	long grain rice	250 mL
½ tsp	dried thyme OR 1 tsp/5 mL fresh thyme	2 mL
½ tsp	dried oregano OR 1 tsp/5 mL fresh oregano	2mL
1	lemon, juice and rind	1
1¼ cups	chicken stock OR water	425 mL
	Salt and pepper	
1 tsp	finely chopped parsley for garnish	5 mL

In a heavy saucepan, melt butter and mix in onion and rice on medium heat. Cook, stirring often, until onions are soft and rice has become opaque. Stir in herbs, lemon juice and rind, then liquid. Add salt and pepper to taste. Bring to a boil, cover, and reduce heat to low. Do not lift lid for 20 minutes. Toss with a fork to mix. Serve as is or mould to serve.

To mould: Butter a 3 cup (750 mL) mould form such as a jelly or ring mould. Spoon cooked rice into mould and press down firmly. This can be done ahead. To heat, set mould in a pan of hot water halfway up the sides of the mould. Set on medium-high heat, covered, for 20 minutes. Remove from water and place serving plate upside down on top of mould and invert mould onto plate. Garnish with parsley.

Makes 6 servings

The secret to delicious rice is never to peek at it while it is cooking.

Quick Pilaf with Pine Nuts
Judith Finlayson

Rice and pine nuts are a wonderful combination; this a traditional family favourite given to Finlayson by a Greek friend.

1 cup	long grain rice	250 mL
2 cups	chicken stock	500 mL
1 to 2 tbsp	pine nuts	15 to 30 mL
1 tbsp	butter	15 mL
¼ cup	low-fat yogurt	50 mL

In a heavy pot, bring rice and stock to a rapid boil. Turn off heat and let sit for 20 minutes without lifting the cover. Meanwhile, cook the pine nuts in melted butter until nicely browned. When the rice is cooked, toss with yogurt and the pine nut-butter mixture. Serve immediately.

Makes 6 servings

CAKES AND SQUARES

Great for gifts or as a luscious finale to an elegant meal, cakes and squares are among those treats that qualify as special rewards.

Wine and Dessert
Tony Aspler

I have not given specific suggestions for wines with the dessert recipes because I fear I would repeat myself too often. The main principle to remember when choosing a wine to accompany dessert is that the wine has to be sweeter than the dish, otherwise it will taste thin and acidic.

Chocolate is a difficult taste to match, and wines should be avoided unless you want to serve port, cream sherry, or a Californian orange muscat liqueur. Bananas, too, are hard to pair off.

The best desserts to match with wines are those that contain fruit with some acidity — apples, pears, plums, peaches, apricots, and red and green berries go wonderfully with sweet wines, especially Canada's Icewines. For fruit-based desserts choose late harvest Rieslings, sauternes, Asti Spumante, or sweet champagne. Or just serve a glass of sweet wine by itself as a dessert.

Brazil Loaves
Margaret Fraser

Great for holiday gift-giving, especially when wrapped in red or green cellophane and tied with ribbon and a sprig of holly. Refrigerate them beforehand for easier slicing. Thanks to the Canadian Living Cookbook *for this fruit-filled confection.*

3 cups	halved, pitted dates (about 1 lb/500 g)	750 mL
1 cup	candied pineapple chunks	250 mL
1 cup	mixed red and green glacé cherries	250 mL
3 cups	unsalted Brazil nuts (about 1 lb/500 g)	750 mL
1 cup	all-purpose flour	250 mL
1 cup	granulated sugar	250 mL
1 tsp	baking powder	5 mL
¼ tsp	salt	1 mL
4	eggs	4
1 tsp	vanilla OR rum extract	5 mL

Line two 9- x 5-inch (2 L) loaf pans with foil; grease well. In large bowl, mix dates, pineapple, cherries, and nuts. In separate bowl, stir together flour, sugar, baking powder, and salt. Add to fruit and nuts. Beat eggs well; stir in vanilla. Add to floured fruit and nuts. Mix well. Spoon batter into prepared pans. Bake at 350°F (180°C) for 1 hour. Cool in pans for 10 minutes, then remove and cool on racks. When cool, wrap tightly in foil or plastic wrap.

Makes 2 loaves

Lemon Cake
Margo Oliver

This is a special cake indeed — its texture is like pound cake, it keeps well and freezes perfectly, it's welcome at cottage or picnic, and it tastes wonderful.

⅔ cup	soft butter	150 mL
2 cups	granulated sugar	500 mL
4	eggs	4
3 cups	sifted all-purpose flour	750 mL
2 tsp	baking powder	10 mL
1 tsp	salt	5 mL
1 cup	milk	250 mL
3 tbsp	grated lemon rind	50 mL
1 cup	finely ground blanched almonds	250 mL
Topping:		
2 tbsp	lemon juice	25 mL
¼ cup	granulated sugar	50 mL
	Icing sugar	

Heat oven to 350°F (180°C). Grease a 10-inch (4 L) tube pan. Beat butter and 2 cups (500 mL) sugar together until light and fluffy (medium speed on the mixer). Add eggs one at a time, beating well after each addition. Sift flour, baking powder, and salt together. Add to first mixture alternately with milk, stirring just to blend after each addition. Fold in lemon rind and almonds. Spoon into pan and bake until a toothpick inserted into the centre comes out clean, about 1¼ hours.

Topping: While cake bakes, combine lemon juice and granulated sugar. Let stand in a warm place and stir occasionally. Leave cake in pan 10 minutes after it comes out of oven, then prick top in several places with the tines of a fork. Drizzle lemon mixture over top slowly, letting it soak in. Cool cake in pan, then invert on plate. Sift icing sugar over cake before serving.

Makes 12 servings

Chocolate Roll
Carol Ferguson

Ferguson's grandmother used to make this flourless cake. It's moist, dark, not too sweet, and still the best and easiest chocolate roll ever.

5	eggs, separated	5
½ cup	granulated sugar	125 mL
½ cup	unsweetened cocoa powder	125 mL
1 tsp	vanilla	5 mL
¼ tsp	cream of tartar	1 mL
1 cup	whipping cream	250 mL

Line a 15- x 10-inch (2 L) jelly-roll pan with waxed paper. Grease the paper. Beat egg yolks lightly; add sugar, cocoa, and vanilla; beat until smooth. Beat egg whites with cream of tartar to stiff peaks. Fold chocolate mixture gently but thoroughly into whites. Spread evenly in pan. Bake at 350°F (180°C) for 15 to 20 minutes or until cake springs back when touched on top. Cool cake in pan 5 minutes, then invert onto tea towel sprinkled with fruit sugar or icing sugar. Peel off paper. Roll cake up in tea towel, starting at narrow end. Let cool completely. Whip cream, adding a few drops of vanilla and a little sugar to taste. Unroll cake, spread with cream, and roll up again. Dust top with icing sugar and cut in slices.

Makes about 8 servings (or 4 with seconds, which is more likely)

Swiss Chocolate Layered Mousse Cake
Dufflet

Chocolate lovers will find this a cake to die for. Serve it for a special dinner party or birthday.

8 oz	soft butter	250 g
1½ cups	granulated sugar	375 mL
2	egg whites	2
2 cups	sifted cake flour	500 mL
2½ tsp	baking powder	12 mL
¼ tsp	salt	1 mL
1 cup	milk	250 mL
1 tsp	vanilla	5 mL
3	egg whites	3
1 tsp	sugar	5 mL

Syrup:

½ cup	water	125 mL
¼ cup	granulated sugar	50 mL
	Liquor (optional)	

Mousse:

1 lb	semisweet Swiss chocolate	500 g
⅔ lb	butter	330 mL
8	egg yolks	8
2 tsp	unflavoured gelatin	10 mL
8	egg whites	8
½ cup	granulated sugar	125 mL
1 cup	whipping cream	250 mL

is a Toronto baker who began Dufflet Pastries in 1975 out of her mom's kitchen. Today, Dufflet supplies more than 250 restaurants, fine food shops, caterers, hotels, and cafés.

Heat oven to 400°F (200°C). Butter and flour two 9-inch (1.5 L) round cake pans. Line with paper.

Cake: Cream butter with mixer until fluffy. Add sugar and continue creaming. Add egg whites and continue to cream until very light. Sift together flour, baking powder, and salt in a separate bowl. Add milk, vanilla, and dry ingredients alternately with butter mixture. End with flour. Mix until combined. Whip 3 egg whites in a separate bowl until soft peaks form. Add 1 tsp (5 mL) sugar and whip until stiff. Fold carefully into flour and butter mixture until whites are incorporated. Divide batter into pans and bake approximately 25 to 30 minutes until tester inserted in centre comes out dry and cake pulls away from sides of pan. Remove from oven and cool on rack.

Syrup: Bring ½ cup (125 mL) water and ¼ cup (50 mL) sugar to boil. Cool. At this point you may add a little liquor.

Mousse: Melt chocolate and butter together and cool to room temperature. Blend egg yolks into chocolate mixture. Dissolve gelatin according to package instructions and add to chocolate mixture. Whip 8 egg whites in clean dry bowl until soft peaks form. Add ½ cup (125 mL) sugar to whites and beat until stiff. Fold into chocolate mixture carefully. Whip cream until very stiff. Fold into chocolate mixture.

Assembly: Slice cooled cakes lengthwise into two halves. Place one half into a 9-inch (2.5 L) springform pan. Brush with syrup. Top with 1 cup (250 mL) mousse. Repeat. Before icing top and sides, refrigerate until mousse has reset. Unmold cake and ice top and sides with remaining mousse. Decorate all over, or just top with chocolate curls (grate a slab of chocolate with a vegetable peeler).

Viennese Plum Cake
Rita Feutl

Feutl's family hails from Austria, where dessert is front and centre. This recipe is from Feutl's mother, who trained in a Viennese bakery (lucky woman!).

½ cup	unsalted butter	125 mL
1 ¼ cups	granulated sugar	425 mL
5	eggs	5
1 tsp	vanilla	5 mL
1 ¼ cups	all-purpose flour	300 mL
½ cup	ground almonds	125 mL
1 tsp	baking powder	5 mL
40 (approx)	plums to fill half a cookie sheet	40
	Cinnamon	

Rita Feutl is the food editor of the *Edmonton* Sun.

Heat oven to 325°F (160°C). Whip butter and sugar together, then add the eggs one by one, whipping after each addition. Add vanilla. Combine flour, almonds, and baking powder; add to egg mixture. Pour onto a buttered cookie sheet. Halve and pit each plum and place, cut side up, in rows on the cookie sheet. Sprinkle with cinammon and bake until the top is golden brown, about 30 to 40 minutes. Cut into largish squares and serve on a platter with generous dollops of whipped cream.

Note: You may also bake this in two large flan dishes, arranging the plums in circles.

Chocolate Bundt Cake
Daphna Rabinovitch

This cake is so dense and satisfying that it requires no topping except a sprinkling of icing sugar.

3 cups	all-purpose flour	750 mL
3 cups	granulated sugar	750 mL
1 cup	unsweetened cocoa powder, sifted	250 mL
1 tbsp	baking powder	15 mL
1 tsp	salt	5 mL
1 cup	unsalted butter, room temperature	250 mL
1 ½ cups	milk	375 mL
1 tbsp	vanilla	15 mL
3	eggs	3
¼ cup	light cream	50 mL
	Icing sugar (optional)	

In large bowl, sift together flour, sugar, cocoa, baking powder, and salt; stir until well mixed. Make a well in centre of flour mixture. Add butter, milk, and vanilla. With electric beaters, beat mixture for 5 minutes or until very light and fluffy. Add eggs one at a time, beating well after each addition. Beat in cream. Scrape mixture into well-greased 10-inch (3 L) bundt pan. Bake at 325°F (160°C) 1 ½ hours or until cake tester inserted in centre comes out clean and cake springs back when lightly pressed. When cooled, sprinkle with icing sugar (optional).

Makes 12 to 16 servings

Apple Cake with Caramel Pecan Sauce
Daphna Rabinovitch

A moist and chunky apple cake that's heavenly served warm. Don't forget that scoop of vanilla ice cream.

1 cup	unsalted butter, room temperature	250 mL
1 cup	granulated sugar	250 mL
2	eggs	2
1½ tsp	vanilla	7 mL
1½ cups	all-purpose flour	625 mL
1½ tsp	cinnamon	7 mL
1 tsp	baking soda	5 mL
¼ tsp	grated nutmeg	1 mL
¼ tsp	allspice	1 mL
3	tart apples, peeled, cored, and chopped	3
1 cup	chopped pecans	250 mL
Sauce:		
¼ cup	unsalted butter	50 mL
½ cup	pecan halves	125 mL
1 cup	packed light brown sugar	250 mL
¾ cup	whipping cream	175 mL

In bowl with electric mixer, beat together butter and sugar until light and fluffy. Beat in eggs one at a time, beating well after each addition; beat in vanilla. Sift together flour, cinnamon, baking soda, nutmeg, and allspice. On low speed, beat flour mixture into egg mixture. Stir in apples and pecans. Scrape mixture into greased 9-inch (2.5 L) springform pan. Bake at 350°F (180°C) for 35 to 45 minutes or until cake tester inserted in centre comes out clean and cake springs back when lightly pressed. Cool in pan for 10 minutes; unmold and cool on rack.

   Sauce: In saucepan over medium high heat, melt butter. Add nuts and cook, stirring, for 8 to 10 minutes or until the butter is lightly browned. Add the brown sugar and cream; bring to a boil. Boil until mixture is slightly reduced and thickened, about 10 minutes. (Sauce can be made up to 5 days in advance and rewarmed over low heat before serving.) Slice cake and serve sauce separately.

Makes 8 servings

Chocolate Almond Cake
Julia Aitken

A little of this fudgy cake goes a long way. Be sure not to overcook it because it should be a little moist at its centre.

6	squares semisweet chocolate, coarsely chopped	6
⅓ cup	softened unsalted butter	75 mL
¼ cup	granulated sugar	50 mL
3	eggs, separated	3
¾ cup	ground almonds	175 mL
1¼ cups	fresh white bread crumbs	425 mL
	Whipped cream	
	Toasted sliced almonds	

Grease an 8-inch (2 L) springform cake pan, line base with a circle of waxed paper; set aside. In medium bowl over saucepan of hot (not boiling) water, melt chocolate, stirring occasionally, until smooth. Or, microwave at Medium (50%) power 2 minutes, stirring once. Remove from heat; let cool slightly. In large bowl and using electric mixer, cream butter and sugar until light and fluffy. Beat in egg yolks, one at a time, beating well after each addition. Beat in chocolate and ground almonds. Stir in bread crumbs. With clean dry beaters, beat egg whites until they hold stiff peaks. Fold one-quarter of egg whites into chocolate mixture to lighten it. Fold in remaining egg whites until well combined. Spoon mixture into cake pan. Bake at 350°F (180°C) for 20 to 25 minutes or until centre of cake springs back when lightly touched. Do not overcook; cake should still be moist. Run a knife around edge of cake pan. Let cake cool in pan on wire rack. Remove from pan. Serve at room temperature, garnished with rosettes of whipped cream and toasted sliced almonds.

Makes 8 servings

To toast almonds, spread on baking sheet. Bake at 350°F (180°C) for 5 to 7 minutes or until golden and fragrant.

Birthday Chocolate Layer Cake
Carroll Allen

What makes this "birthdayish" is its homemade goodness, perfect for that special celebration for someone you love.

½ cup	softened shortening OR margarine	125 mL
2 cups	packed brown sugar	500 mL
2	eggs	2
1½ cups (generous)	sifted all-purpose flour	375 mL
½ cup	unsweetened cocoa	125 mL
1 tsp	baking powder	5 mL
⅔ tsp	salt	3 mL
1 tsp	baking soda	5 mL
½ cup	boiling water	125 mL
½ cup	sour milk OR fresh milk with a few drops of vinegar added	125 mL

Butter Mocha Icing:

3 tbsp	softened butter	50 mL
1½ tbsp	unsweetened cocoa	20 mL
2 to 3 cups	icing sugar	500 to 750 mL
2 to 3 tbsp	strong coffee	25 to 50 mL

Beat together shortening, sugar, and eggs until light and fluffy. Sift together flour, cocoa, baking powder, and salt. Mix baking soda and boiling water. Add dry ingredients to shortening mixture alternately with hot water and sour milk, beating to keep mixture smooth. Pour into two oiled 9-inch (1.5 L) round cake pans and bake at 350°F (180°C) for 25 minutes or until a toothpick inserted in the centre comes out clean. Cool on racks.

Icing: Cream the butter and cocoa together. Start adding icing sugar alternately with coffee and beat until you get the quantity of icing you want, of a consistency to spread. Sandwich cakes together with icing and spread rest of icing over top and sides.

Makes 12 to 18 servings

Carroll Allen is an award-winning food writer who has also been food editor of Homemaker's *and* Recipes Only *magazines.*

Hazelnut Torte
Pam Collacott

Collacott says this continues to be a smashing and popular cake. In addition, it freezes beautifully. Have one on hand so you can thaw it and decorate it with whipped cream and whole toasted hazelnuts at virtually a moment's notice.

Cake:

4	eggs	4
¾ cup	granulated sugar	175 mL
2 tbsp	all-purpose flour	25 mL
2 ½ tsp	baking powder	12 mL
1 cup	hazelnuts	250 mL

Filling:

2 tbsp	soft unsalted butter	25 mL
1 to 1 ½ cups	icing sugar	250 to 375 mL
1 tsp	unsweetened cocoa	5 mL
1 tbsp	strong coffee	15 mL
½ tsp	vanilla	2 mL

Topping:

1 cup	whipping cream, whipped	250 mL
8 to 10	whole hazelnuts	8 to 10
	Unsweetened cocoa	

Butter and flour two 9-inch (1.5 L) round cake pans. Heat oven to 350°F (180°C).

Cake: In food processor or blender, process all cake ingredients until hazelnuts are finely chopped. Pour half of batter into each prepared pan and bake for 20 minutes or until a toothpick inserted in the centre comes out clean. Cool cakes completely on wire racks.

Filling: Cream together butter and 1 cup (250 mL) icing sugar. Add coffee, cocoa, and vanilla and beat until smooth. If too thin to spread, add more icing sugar. Place first cake layer on serving plate. Spread with filling and top with second layer. Wrap well in plastic wrap and freeze if desired, or coat top and sides with whipped cream. Arrange hazelnuts on top, then dust with cocoa shaken gently through a fine sieve. Serve at once or refrigerate.

Makes 8 to 10 servings

Strawberry Rhubarb Linzer Pie
Dufflet

This almond crust filled with strawberries and rhubarb is a delicious variation on the traditional Linzertorte.

Crust:

1 cup	chilled butter	250 mL
1 cup	granulated sugar	250 mL
2 cups	all-purpose flour	500 mL
9 oz	ground almonds	260 mL
½ tsp	cinnamon	2 mL
Pinch	ground cloves	Pinch
2	egg yolks	2

Filling:

1 oz	butter	30 mL
1 ¼ lb	fresh rhubarb, OR frozen (thawed), cut into ½-inch (1 cm) pieces	625 mL
¼ cup	granulated sugar	50 mL
1 tbsp	cornstarch	15 mL
½ lb	strawberries	250 mL
1	fresh orange rind, finely grated	1

Heat oven to 400°F (200°C). Butter 10-inch (25 cm) springform pan.

Crust: Cut chilled butter into small pieces. Add sugar to butter in food processor and blend until creamy. Add flour, almonds, cinnamon, and cloves until it gets crumbly. Combine egg yolks with above until mixture holds together. Use hands if necessary. Refrigerate 1 ½ hours. Prepare the filling.

Filling: Melt 1 oz (30 mL) butter and ¼ cup (50 mL) sugar in large pot. Stir rhubarb into above and cook over medium heat until tender. Strain off juice, reserve. Keep rhubarb on stove at low heat. Add cornstarch to rhubarb juice and mix. Add sugar to rhubarb juice and mix. Stir this into rhubarb and cook until thickened. Stir strawberries and orange rind into above and remove from heat. Cool.

Assembly: Remove dough from refrigerator and, when soft enough, take two-thirds and press into bottom and sides of pan with fingers. Pour filling into crust. Crumble remaining dough on top of filling. Bake 15 minutes and lower oven temperature to 325°F (160°C) for another 20 minutes or until crust is golden brown. Cool completely before serving.

Makes 16 servings

Matrimony Cake
Carroll Allen

The western term is much more romantic than the eastern Canadian version — date squares. Allen says this was one of her favourite childhood treats and was also loved by her own children.

1 cup	all-purpose flour	250 mL
1 tsp	baking soda	5 mL
1 cup	packed brown sugar	250 mL
2 cups	rolled oats	500 mL
¾ cup	softened butter OR margarine	200 mL
Filling:		
2 cups	pitted and chopped dates	500 mL
⅓ cup	packed brown sugar	75 mL
1 ¼ cups	water	300 mL
1 tbsp	all-purpose flour	15 mL
1 tsp	vanilla	5 mL

Combine flour, baking soda, 1 cup (250 mL) brown sugar, rolled oats, and butter in a medium mixing bowl. Rub together with fingers until it resembles coarse meal.

Filling: Combine filling ingredients in a saucepan and simmer, stirring constantly, until slightly thickened. Press half the flour mixture into the bottom of a greased 9-inch (2.5 L) square cake pan. Spoon filling on top and smooth with the back of a spoon. Sprinkle remaining flour mixture evenly on top. Bake at 375°F (190°C) for about 25 minutes, until top is slightly browned. Cool in pan and cut into squares.

Makes 16 servings

COOKIES, MUFFINS AND BISCUITS

There's nothing like the smell of baking in the oven to evoke the fondest of childhood memories. Cookies or muffins or biscuits are the ultimate comfort food. With a glass of milk or a cup of hot chocolate or tea, they can brighten up the darkest day.

Oatmeal Shortbread
Margaret Fraser

My mother made real Scottish shortbread the 1-2-4 way: 1 cup sugar, 2 cups butter, and 4 cups flour. But when I co-authored The Total Fibre Book, *I felt less guilty eating shortbread with oatmeal added, even if it was still a little high in fat.*

1 cup	butter	250 mL
¾ cup	packed brown sugar	175 mL
2 tsp	vanilla	10 mL
2 cups	all-purpose flour	500 mL
1 cup	rolled oats	250 mL

Cream together butter and sugar; blend in vanilla. Gradually work in flour and oatmeal, using a spoon or your fingers. Chill for about 20 minutes or until firm enough to roll. Roll out on lightly floured surface, to about ¼ inch (5 mm) thickness. Cut into 2-inch (5 cm) rounds. Place on ungreased cookie sheets; prick with fork. Bake at 325°F (160°C) for 20 minutes or until lightly browned.

Makes about 4 dozen

Mocha Shortbread
Elizabeth Baird

This is an excellent twist on traditional shortbread because of a hint of crunch from the fresh coffee grounds.

1 cup	butter, softened	250 mL
½ cup	icing sugar	125 mL
2 tsp	strong brewed coffee	10 mL
1 to 2 tsp	vanilla	5 to 10 mL
¼ tsp	almond extract	1 mL
2⅓ cups	all-purpose flour	575 mL
1 tbsp	unsweetened cocoa powder	15 mL
1 tbsp	medium-ground coffee	15 mL
¼ tsp	salt	1 mL
¼ cup	granulated sugar	50 mL

In bowl, cream butter with icing sugar until fluffy; beat in liquid coffee, vanilla, and almond extract. Stir together flour, cocoa powder, ground coffee, and salt. Blend into butter mixture, using hands if necessary. On waxed paper, shape into rectangle about 2 inches (5 cm) wide and 1 inch (2.5 cm) thick. Cut into ½-inch (1 cm) slices. Bake on ungreased cookie sheets at 350°F (180°C) for about 20 minutes or until firm and lightly browned on bottom. Press gently into granulated sugar. Let cool on racks. Store in airtight containers at room temperature for up to 2 weeks.

Makes about 30 cookies

Double Fudge Cookies
Daphna Rabinovitch

Bet you can't eat just one. These rich and addictive cookies have been known not to even make it to the oven.

10 oz	semisweet chocolate, coarsely chopped	300 g
1 cup	packed brown sugar	250 mL
1 cup	granulated sugar	250 mL
1 cup	unsalted butter, room temperature	250 mL
2	eggs	2
1 tsp	vanilla	5 mL
1¾ cup	all-purpose flour	425 mL
1 tsp	baking soda	5 mL
1 cup	semisweet chocolate chips	250 mL

In food processor, combine semisweet chocolate and brown and white sugars; process until powder fine, scraping down sides of bowl twice. Cut in butter; process for 30 seconds or until well combined. Add eggs and vanilla and process for 30 seconds or until well combined, scraping down sides of bowl once. Sift together the flour and baking soda. Add the flour mixture and chocolate chips to food processor; pulse 10 to 12 times, scraping down sides of bowl once. Transfer cookie dough to bowl; cover and refrigerate overnight or until firm (about 4 hours). Unbaked cookie dough can be made ahead and refrigerated for up to 5 days. Form balls with cookie dough — the size of the ball will depend on the size of cookie you prefer; they can be as small as 1 inch (2.5 cm) or as large as an ice cream scoop — and place at least 2 inches (5 cm) apart on greased cookie sheets. Bake at 350°F (180°C) for about 15 minutes for 3-inch (8 cm) cookies. Cook until the cookies have set but the centre is still soft. Cool on racks. Store in airtight containers for up to four days.

Makes about 35 3-inch (8 cm) cookies

 Never substitute a compound chocolate. Always use semisweet pure chocolate.

Brandy Snaps
Julian Armstrong

This British treat is my mother's recipe and dates back at least to the turn of the century in her family. Try them plain for afternoon tea or filled with lightly sweetened whipped cream for dessert. (Add a favourite fruit salad and you've a special ending for a dinner party.)

½ cup	molasses	125 mL
½ cup	butter OR margarine	125 mL
1 cup	all-purpose flour	250 mL
⅔ cup	granulated sugar	150 mL
1 tsp	ground ginger, or more to taste	5 mL
1 tsp	lemon juice	5 mL
¼ tsp	vanilla OR 2 tsp (10 mL) brandy	2 mL

Heat molasses and butter together in a saucepan, stirring until blended. Remove from heat. Sift together the flour, sugar, and ginger and stir into the hot molasses mixture, blending well. Add lemon juice and vanilla extract. (This mixture can be made in advance and refrigerated until you are ready to bake the snaps.) Drop batter by half-teaspoonfuls (or heaping teaspoonfuls for a large size) three to four inches (8 to 10 cm) apart on greased cookie sheets. Bake at 300°F (150°C) one sheetful at a time, for five to eight minutes, or until batter spreads out and bubbles appear all over the surface. Quickly remove cookie sheet from oven and loosen snaps, one at a time, with a spatula and roll each over the handle of a wooden spoon. Let stand until dry and set, then slip off onto a rack. You will probably need to do a test batch until you become expert. If the snaps harden on the cookie sheet, you can return the sheet to the oven briefly until they soften again.

Makes about 50 small snaps, or 36 large ones

Thumbprint Cookies
Bonnie Stern

Think shortbreads and tiny jam tarts and you get the idea behind these pretty cookies. Kids love helping to make the thumbprint holes.

1 cup	unsalted butter	250 mL
⅓ cup	packed light brown sugar	75 mL
⅓ cup	granulated sugar	75 mL
2	egg yolks	2
1 tsp	vanilla	5 mL
2¼ cups	all-purpose flour	550 mL
Pinch	salt	Pinch
2	egg whites	2
1½ cups	finely chopped pecans, hazelnuts, OR almonds	375 mL
1 cup (approx)	assorted jams OR jellies	250 mL

Heat oven to 350°F (180°C). Butter and lightly flour cookie sheets or line with parchment paper. Cream butter until light. Beat in brown and granulated sugars. Add egg yolks and vanilla and beat until well blended. Combine flour with salt and add to batter. Stir just until dough is formed. Shape cookies into 1-inch (2.5 cm) balls, place on a tray, and refrigerate while assembling other ingredients. Lightly beat egg white in a shallow bowl. Place finely chopped nuts in another shallow dish. Roll each ball of cookie dough in egg white and then lightly in nuts. Place on prepared pans about 1 inch (2.5 cm) apart. Press centre of each cookie slightly to make an indentation for the jam. Bake for 9 to 12 minutes, or until cookies are lightly browned. If centres have risen slightly, gently press indentation again. Cool on racks. When cookies are cool, spoon a little jam or jelly into the centres.

Makes approximately 50 cookies

Chocolate Mint Cookies
Julie Cohen

Julie Cohen is an editor and writer with more than ten years experience in corporate communications, magazine editing, and copywriting. She currently operates her own copywriting business and has written about food for many publications.

This recipe came from my grandmother, who passed it on to my aunt by letter. It is one of the better uses I know of for Rice Krispies®.

½ cup	butter	125 mL
½ cup	packed brown sugar	125 mL
¼ cup	granulated sugar	50 mL
1	egg	1
1 tsp	vanilla	5 mL
½ cup	Rice Krispies®	125 mL
1 cup	all-purpose flour	250 mL
½ tsp	baking soda	2 mL
½ cup	semisweet chocolate chips	125 mL
½ cup	semisweet mint chocolate chips	125 mL
½ cup	Thompson seedless raisins, tossed in flour	125 mL

In large bowl, cream together butter and sugars. Add egg, vanilla, and Rice Krispies®. Mix to blend. Then add flour, soda, both types of chocolate chips, and raisins. Stir to combine; the mixture will be quite thick. Drop tablespoonfuls on ungreased cookie sheets and bake at 350°F (180°C) for 10 minutes. Loosen from pan at once and let cool on sheet.

Makes about three dozen cookies

Mint chips are available in bulk food warehouses or in the baking departments of supermarkets.

The Best Apple Pie Muffins Ever
Daphna Rabinovitch

It's not just the crumbly tops that are so good. Lots of apple and a buttermilk batter on the bottoms make the difference, too.

Topping:

½ cup	packed brown sugar	125 mL
⅓ cup	all-purpose flour	75 mL
¼ cup	unsalted butter, melted	50 mL
1 tsp	cinnamon	5 mL

Muffins:

1½ cups	packed light brown sugar	375 mL
⅔ cup	vegetable oil	150 mL
1	egg	1
1½ tsp	vanilla	7 mL
2½ cups	all-purpose flour	625 mL
1 tsp	baking soda	5 mL
¼ tsp	salt	1 mL
1 cup	buttermilk	250 mL
2 cups	diced, peeled, firm, tart apples (such as Spy, Granny Smith)	500 mL

Topping: In small bowl, toss together sugar, flour, butter, and cinnamon until crumbly. Set aside.

Muffins: In large bowl, whisk together brown sugar, oil, egg, and vanilla until smooth. In separate bowl, sift together flour, soda, and salt. Stir oil mixture into flour mixture alternately with buttermilk. Fold in apple, mixing just until combined. Spoon into greased muffin cups, filling ¾ full. Sprinkle topping over evenly. Bake at 350°F (180°C) for 25 to 30 minutes or until golden brown and tops spring back.

Makes 18 muffins

Spicy Rhubarb Muffins
Rose Murray

These streusel-topped muffins are nice and moist and have a refreshing tartness from bits of rhubarb

Streusel Topping:

¼ cup	chopped pecans	50 mL
¼ cup	all-purpose flour	50 mL
¼ cup	granulated sugar	50 mL
¼ cup	butter	50 mL

Muffins:

3	eggs	3
1 cup	vegetable oil	250 mL
2 cups	packed light brown sugar	500 mL
1½ tsp	vanilla	7 mL
2½ cups	finely diced rhubarb	625 mL
½ cup	chopped pecans	125 mL
3 cups	all-purpose flour	750 mL
2 tsp	baking soda	10 mL
½ tsp	baking powder	2 mL
1½ tsp	cinnamon	7 mL
½ tsp	salt	2 mL
½ tsp	allspice	2 mL
½ tsp	nutmeg	2 mL

Streusel Topping: In food processor, chop pecans finely and add flour, sugar, and butter; process until fine.

Muffins: In large bowl, beat together eggs, oil, sugar, and vanilla until thick and foamy. Stir in rhubarb and nuts. In another bowl, stir together flour, baking soda, baking powder, cinnamon, salt, allspice, and nutmeg. Gradually add to rhubarb mixture, stirring gently just to blend. Spoon into 24 greased muffin cups. Sprinkle some of the streusel topping over each muffin and bake at 350°F (180°C) for 25 to 30 minutes or until tester inserted in centre comes out clean.

Makes 24 muffins

 If fresh rhubarb is unavailable, substitute frozen, defrosted and drained.

Jessie's Biscuits
Anita Stewart

Jessie Eakett dictated this recipe to Anita Stewart's son when she was 92 years old. She farmed in Grey County during the early 1900s and made everything from produce grown on her property. When the trees were tapped each spring and the maple sap boiled down to syrup, it was poured over these biscuits.

2 cups	all-purpose flour	500 mL
1 tbsp	baking powder	15 mL
Pinch	salt	Pinch
1 tbsp	granulated sugar	15 mL
¼ to ⅓ cup	shortening OR lard	50 to 75 mL
½ cup (or more)	raisins	250 mL
1 ⅓ cups	milk	325 mL

The oven should be about 400° to 425°F (200° to 220°C). The hotter it is, the faster the biscuits will bake. Mix together with your hands until it's sort of crumbly. Add as many raisins as you'd like. Then stir in some milk — about 1 ⅓ cups (325 mL). The dough shouldn't be sticky. Roll or pat quickly into a round, on a floured surface. Cut into wedges or small biscuits with a sharp tumbler you've dipped in flour. Bake on a greased cookie sheet for 15 to 25 minutes or until they begin to brown around the edges. Serve hot with butter and maple syrup, homemade jam or honey.

Makes enough biscuits for 6 to 8 people

Anita Stewart is the author of several cookbooks, including From Our Mothers' Kitchens. *A contributor to many newspapers and magazines, she lives in Elora, Ontario.*

Whole-Wheat Seed Scones
Jan Main

These can be made in minutes to serve for breakfast with marmalade or for lunch or supper with soups. They're always a hit and worth the bit of extra work "from scratch."

1 cup	cake flour	250 mL
1 cup	whole-wheat flour	250 mL
2 to 4 tbsp	mixture of seeds such as sesame, poppy, sunflower OR pumpkin (unsalted)	25 to 50 mL
1 tbsp	granulated sugar	15 mL
2 tsp	baking powder	10 mL
½ tsp	baking soda	2 mL
½ tsp	salt	2 mL
½ cup	shortening	125 mL
1 cup	grated old Cheddar cheese	250 mL
¾ cup	yogurt OR milk, OR buttermilk OR mixture of yogurt and milk	300 mL
1	egg	1
	Additional seeds and grated cheese	

In large bowl, combine flours, seeds, sugar, baking powder, baking soda, and salt. Cut in shortening, using 2 knives or a pastry blender, until mixture is a coarse crumb consistency. Stir cheese into flour mixture. Stir liquid ingredients into flour mixture just until moistened. Spoon dough onto a lightly floured piece of waxed paper and with floured hands pat into a rectangle about 1 inch (2.5 cm) high. Using 2-inch (5 cm) cookie cutters, cut into circles and place on a greased baking sheet. If you wish, brush the biscuits with a mixture of beaten egg and a tablespoon (15 cm) of water and sprinkle with seeds and a little cheese. Bake at 425°F (220°C) for 12 to 15 minutes or until golden brown. Serve hot or at room temperature. These freeze well in freezer containers for up to 6 months.

Makes 8 to 12 scones

PIES, PUDDINGS, AND COBBLERS

There is something quintessential about a freshly baked pie cooling on a countertop. Smooth and soothing, puddings and cobblers have an old-fashioned air. These tantalizing recipes add some twists to old favourites.

Mocha Pie
Iris Raven

Compliments are guaranteed with this light and tantalizing pie.

3	eggs, separated	3
½ cup	granulated sugar	125 mL
½ cup	unsweetened cocoa	125 mL
1 tbsp	instant coffee granules (freeze-dried)	15 mL
1	envelope unflavoured gelatin	1
1 cup	milk	250 mL
1 tbsp	coffee liqueur OR 1 tsp (5 mL) vanilla	15 mL
Pinch	cream of tartar	Pinch
½ cup	whipping cream	125 mL
1	baked 9-inch (23 cm) pie shell	1

Topping:

2 tbsp	unsweetened cocoa	30 mL
1 tbsp	boiling water	15 mL
2 tsp	instant coffee granules	10 mL
1 tsp	vanilla	5 mL
1	egg white, reserved	1
Pinch	cream of tartar	Pinch
2 tbsp	granulated sugar	30 mL
½ cup	whipping cream	125 mL

Separate eggs, reserving one of the egg whites for topping. Measure ⅓ cup (75 mL) sugar into heavy saucepan. Stir in cocoa, coffee granules, and gelatine. Whisk in milk and egg yolks. Cook, stirring, over medium heat until thick enough to coat back of metal spoon, about 5 minutes. Do not boil. Stir in liqueur or vanilla. Chill, covered, stirring occasionally until consistency of thick custard, about 35 minutes.

In large bowl, add cream of tartar to 2 egg whites. Beat until soft peaks form. Gradually beat in remaining sugar until stiff peaks form. In separate bowl, beat whipping cream until just stiff. Stir beaten egg whites into whipped cream. Beat cocoa mixture to lighten. Stir in about a quarter of whipped cream mixture; fold in remainder. Turn into baked shell. Set aside.

Topping: Blend together cocoa and boiling water in small bowl. Stir in coffee granules and vanilla. Set aside. In separate bowl, beat egg white with cream of tartar until soft peaks form. Do not overbeat. Gradually beat in sugar until stiff peaks form. In large bowl, beat cream until just stiff. Fold cocoa mixture into whipped cream. Fold egg white into cream mixture. Spread over filling in pie shell. Chill for at least 1 hour before serving.

Makes 8 servings

Chocolate Pecan Pie
Rose Reisman

Not only is this an excellent marriage of tastes, it's also simple to make, even for non-bakers.

Crust:		
1 ½ cups	all-purpose flour	375 mL
⅓ cup	icing sugar	75 mL
6 oz	butter	150 g

Filling:		
3 oz	semisweet chocolate	75 g
1 oz	butter	25 g
1 cup	corn syrup	250 mL
1 cup	granulated sugar	250 mL
3	eggs	3
1 cup	pecan halves	250 mL
¼ cup	small semisweet chocolate chips (optional)	50 mL

Heat oven to 350°F (180°C). Butter a 9 to 10-inch (23 to 25 cm) pie plate or flan pan.

Crust: Combine flour and icing sugar in food processor. Add butter until ball forms. Pat into bottom and sides of pan. Bake approximately 15 to 20 minutes until slightly brown. Cool.

Filling: Melt chocolate and butter and stir until smooth. Set aside. Heat corn syrup and sugar until easy to mix. Add chocolate mixture and blend well. Add eggs until combined. Add pecan halves and chocolate chips and combine. Pour into crust and bake approximately 45 minutes. Centre will remain soft. Cool.

Makes 6 to 8 servings

 Melt chocolate in microwave at defrost for 3 minutes, or until chocolate begins to melt. Or melt in top of double boiler over, not in, hot water for 10 to 12 minutes.

Sour Cream Apple Pie
Rose Reisman

A mouth-watering combination — this may be the best apple pie in the world.

Crust:

1 ½ cups	graham cracker crumbs	375 mL
½ cup	melted butter	125 mL
¼ cup	granulated sugar	50 mL

Filling:

¾ cup	granulated sugar	175 mL
2 tbsp	all-purpose flour	25 mL
1 cup	sour cream	250 mL
1	egg	1
1 tsp	vanilla	5 mL
¼ tsp	cinnamon	1 mL
5	large apples (best with Granny Smith OR Spy apples)	5

Topping:

3 oz	chopped walnuts	75 g
½ cup	granulated sugar	125 mL
½ tsp	vanilla	2 mL
½ tsp	cinnamon	2 mL
4 oz	butter	100 g
1 ½ cups	all-purpose flour	375 mL

Heat oven to 350°F (180°C). Butter and flour a 9-inch (23 cm) pie plate or springform pan.

Crust: Combine well graham cracker crumbs, melted butter, and sugar and press into pan. Refrigerate.

Filling: Mix sugar, flour, sour cream, egg, vanilla, and cinnamon in large bowl until well combined. Peel and core apples, and slice thinly. Add to above and mix well. Pour into crust and bake 30 minutes.

Topping: Combine all topping ingredients in a food processor just until crumbly. After filling has baked for 30 minutes, sprinkle topping over apple mixture and bake another 15 to 20 minutes. Cool on rack.

Makes 6 to 8 servings

Apricot Peach Pie
Iris Raven

You will love the combination of dried fruits and fresh or canned with a crunchy, nutty streusel on top.

1 cup	packed dried Turkish apricots, cut in halves	250 mL
1	unbaked 9-inch (23 cm) pie shell	1
1	can (19 oz/540 mL) sliced peaches	1
1 tbsp	lemon juice	15 mL
1 tsp	grated lemon rind	5 mL
¼ cup	granulated sugar	60 mL
2 tbsp	cornstarch	30 mL

Streusel topping:

½ cup	sliced almonds	125 mL
¼ cup	granulated sugar	60 mL
¼ cup	all-purpose flour	60 mL
2 tbsp	butter	30 mL

Cover apricots with boiling water in small saucepan and let stand 1 hour.

Crust: Meanwhile, prick pastry shell all over with a fork. Line with parchment or foil and fill with pie weights or dry rice. Bake at 425°F (220°C) for 8 minutes. Remove liner and weights; bake 7 minutes longer or until bottom is dry and firm. Cool on rack.

Filling: Drain apricots; discard liquid. Pour liquid from peaches over apricots; set peaches aside. Add lemon juice and peel to apricots; bring to boil. Cover and simmer until apricots are tender and liquid is reduced by one-third, about 20 minutes. Mix sugar and cornstarch. Blend into apricots and cook until liquid is thickened. Stir in peaches. Cool 5 minutes; spoon into baked pie shell.

Streusel Topping: Stir together almonds, sugar, and flour. Blend in butter with a fork until mixture is crumbly. Sprinkle pie with streusel topping. Bake at 425°F (220°C) for 15 to 20 minutes, or until filling is bubbly and topping is golden brown.

Makes 6 to 8 servings

Golden Pear Pie
Julie V. Watson

By using the microwave you can cut your oven use to the shorter time it takes just for the browning of the pie.

4	fresh, slightly underripe pears,	4
	Bosc OR Anjou, peeled if desired,	
	cored and sliced	
	Lemon juice	
½ cup	dried apricots	125 mL
½ cup	packed brown sugar	125 mL
2 tbsp	all-purpose flour	25 mL
¼ cup	chopped pecans	50 mL
¼ tsp	cinnamon	1 mL
Dash	salt	Dash
	Pastry for a 2-crust 9-inch	
	(23 cm) pie	
2 tbsp	butter OR margarine	25 mL

In bowl, sprinkle pears with lemon juice and set aside. In pot, cover apricots with water. Bring to a boil and simmer 10 minutes. Drain and dice. In separate bowl, combine pears, apricots, brown sugar, flour, pecans, cinnamon, and salt. Turn into pastry-lined pie plate; dot with butter. Adjust top crust, seal and flute edges, and cut vents into top crust.

  Microwave cooking: Microwave at High (100%) for 10 to 12 minutes or until filling is bubbly. Bake in conventional oven at 425°F (220°C) for 10 to 15 minutes or until golden brown.

  Note: This recipe was developed for a 600 to 700 watt microwave oven.

  Oven cooking: Bake at 425°F (220°C) for 45 to 50 minutes or until golden brown.

Makes 6 servings

Bread and Butter Pudding
Thelma Dickman

Thelma Dickman is a renowned travel and food writer, broadcaster, and editor.

Thanks to Anton Mosimann, who gave Dickman this wonderful comfort-food recipe. Though traditional, it has become a favourite nineties ending to a meal in North American restaurants and homes.

¼ cup	golden raisins	50 mL
¼ cup	currants	50 mL
	Rum (optional)	
8	slices stale French bread, ⅓ inch thick	8
3 tbsp	unsalted butter, melted	45 mL
2	large eggs	2
1	large egg yolk	1
¼ cup plus 1 tbsp	granulated sugar	75 mL
3 cups	whipping cream, scalded	750 mL

Heat oven to 300°F (150°C). Soak raisins and currants in rum OR blanch slightly. In a buttered oval 9- by 6- by 3-inch ovenproof dish sprinkle half the raisins and currants. Arrange bread slices over dried fruit, covering bottom of the dish. Cut little bits to fill any holes. Drizzle melted butter over the bread. In large bowl, beat eggs and yolk until combined. Gradually add ¼ cup (50 mL) of the sugar, and beat until mixture ribbons when beaters are lifted. Whisk in scalded cream and strain mixture over the bread. Sprinkle pudding with remaining raisins and currants. Set dish in a baking pan and pour enough hot water into the pan to reach halfway up the sides of the dish. Bake for 1 hour. Remove dish from the pan. Sprinkle pudding with 1 tbsp (15 mL) sugar, and place under broiler for 1 to 2 minutes or until top is golden brown and sugar is caramelized.

Makes 6 to 8 servings

Steamed Ginger Apple Pudding
Judith Comfort

As an alternative to plum pudding at Christmas, this cannot be beaten. Serve it any time of year after a light soup and salad meal. The butterscotch sauce is good on ice cream, too.

¼ cup	butter	50 mL
½ cup	packed brown sugar	125 mL
1	egg	1
½ cup	molasses	125 mL
1 tsp	grated lemon rind	5 mL
½ cup	milk	125 mL
2 tbsp	freshly squeezed lemon juice	25 mL
1 tsp	finely minced stem ginger in heavy syrup	5 mL
1½ cups	all-purpose flour	375 mL
1 tsp	baking powder	5 mL
½ tsp	baking soda	2 mL
½ tsp	freshly grated nutmeg	2 mL
½ tsp	cinnamon	2 mL
1	large apple	1

In large bowl, cream butter and sugar together. Beat in egg, molasses, lemon rind, milk, lemon juice, and ginger. In medium bowl, sift together flour, baking powder, baking soda, nutmeg, and cinnamon. Combine flour and butter mixture. Peel, core, and chop apple and fold into mixture. Pour into 1-quart (1 L) buttered mold and steam 1½ hours. Serve with butterscotch sauce (recipe following).

Butterscotch Sauce:

1	egg	1
3 tbsp	melted butter	45 mL
1 cup	packed brown sugar	250 mL
½ tsp	vanilla	2 mL
1 cup	whipping cream	250 mL

In small bowl, beat together egg, butter, brown sugar, and vanilla. In medium bowl, whip cream, then gently fold egg mixture into whipped cream. Refrigerate until ready to serve.

Makes 8 servings

Judith Comfort is a writer who lives with her family by the sea in Nova Scotia. She's the author of five books on food and travel of the region.

Peach Clafoutis
Nancy Enright

This easy deep-dish recipe comes out puffy and golden brown. It's traditionally made with cherries, but almost any fruit will do nicely.

1 ½ cups	milk	375 mL
4	eggs	4
½ cup	all-purpose flour	125 mL
¼ cup	granulated sugar	50 mL
2 tsp	vanilla	10 mL
1 ½ cups	peeled, sliced peaches	375 mL
	Icing sugar	

In electric blender (or in bowl with whisk) blend milk, eggs, flour, sugar, and vanilla until smooth. Place peaches in bottom of buttered 6-cup (1.5 L) baking dish. Pour batter over top. Bake in middle of 325°F (180°C) oven for 1 ½ hours or until top is puffed and golden brown. Sprinkle with icing sugar. Serve at once.

Makes 4 to 6 servings

Rhubarb Cobbler
Bonnie Stern

This old favourite never goes out of fashion. The mixture may be a bit runny when you take it out of the oven but it will firm up when it cools. If you like, you can add 1 tbsp (15 mL) all-purpose flour to the rhubarb mixture at the start. It calls for a dollop of ice cream and maybe a dusting of icing sugar.

2 lb	rhubarb, cut into 1-inch (2.5 cm) pieces	1 kg
¾ cup	granulated sugar	175 mL
½ cup	packed brown sugar	125 mL
2 tbsp	unsalted butter, cut into bits	25 mL
Topping:		
2 cups	all-purpose flour	500 mL
Pinch	salt	Pinch
1 tbsp	baking powder	15 mL
¼ cup	granulated sugar	50 mL
2 tsp	finely grated orange peel	10 mL
1 tsp	cinnamon	5 mL
½ cup	unsalted butter, cut into pieces	125 mL
1 cup	milk	250 mL

Heat oven to 400°F (200°C). Butter a 12- by 8-inch (3 L) baking dish. In bowl, combine rhubarb with sugars and butter. Spread over bottom of pan.

Topping: In large bowl, combine flour with salt, baking powder, sugar, orange peel, and cinnamon. Cut in butter until it is crumbly. Sprinkle mixture with milk. Stir together just until a heavy batter is formed. Drop batter by spoonfuls over top of rhubarb and spread to cover surface. Bake for 35 to 40 minutes or until biscuit is browned and fruit is tender. Allow to cool before serving.

Makes 8 servings

Use frozen rhubarb if fresh is unavailable. Defrost, then drain off excess liquid.

MORE DESSERTS AND DRINKS

Delectable, these fruit and chocolate desserts are in a class by themselves. They make a memorable finish to any meal. And for special occasions try these special drinks.

Kathy's Lemon Supreme
Julian Armstrong

Armstrong's friend Kathy Keefler gave her name to this lemony chocolate dessert, which can easily be doubled or tripled and can be made 24 hours ahead of serving.

1	envelope unflavoured gelatin	1
1 cup	granulated sugar	250 mL
⅓ cup	cold water	75 mL
	(¼ oz/7 g)	
4	eggs, separated	4
½ tsp	salt	2 mL
	Juice of 2 lemons	
1	square semisweet chocolate	1
1 tsp	shortening	5 mL
1 cup	whipping cream	250 mL

Soften gelatin with ½ cup (125 mL) of the sugar and the water in the top of a double boiler over simmering water. Beat egg yolks slightly in a small bowl. Stir salt and lemon juice into gelatin mixture and add beaten egg yolks. Cook, stirring constantly, until mixture thickens slightly and coats a metal spoon. Strain through a sieve into a large bowl. Cool. Melt chocolate and shortening over simmering water. Beat egg whites until stiff. Sprinkle with remaining ½ cup (125 mL) sugar, a little at a time, beating all the time, until the meringue stands in firm peaks. Whip cream until stiff in another bowl. Have serving bowl ready. Fold meringue into thickened, cooled gelatin mixture. Then fold in whipped cream. Pour about one-third of this mixture into serving bowl. Drizzle with one-third of the chocolate mixture, streaking back and forth over the whole surface. Repeat layers twice more. Chill several hours or until firm.

Makes 6 servings

 Use real lemons in desserts. Do not substitute bottled lemon juice.

Chocolate Marquise
Leslie Lucas

Leslie Lucas until recently operated The Bistro (with Sam Matta), one of the best and friendliest restaurants in Ottawa.

Chocolate lovers rejoice! Here is yet another great dessert to add to your repertoire.

12 oz	bittersweet chocolate	375 g
8 oz	unsalted butter, melted	250 g
6	egg yolks	6
½ cup	granulated sugar	125 mL
½ cup	Dutch process cocoa	125 mL
12	egg whites	12

Sauce Anglaise:

1	fresh vanilla bean	1
2 cups	milk	500 mL
6	egg yolks (room temperature)	6
⅓ cup	granulated sugar	75 mL
	Mint leaves	

Place chocolate in bowl of food processor and chop finely. With motor on, add melted butter and process until smooth. Add egg yolks, sugar, and cocoa and process until combined. Cook over low heat, stirring constantly until sugar dissolves, about 5 minutes. Transfer to a large bowl. In another large dry bowl, whip egg whites to the soft peak stage. Carefully fold whipped egg whites into chocolate mixture and pour into a well-oiled loaf pan. Rap pan on counter to release any trapped air; store, covered with plastic wrap, in refrigerator overnight.

To release the loaf: Cut around the edge with a knife dipped in hot water; cover with a hot towel; invert; tap with a spoon.

Sauce Anglaise: Split vanilla bean and place in saucepan with the milk; bring just to the boil and set aside. Combine egg yolks and sugar and process in food processor. With the motor running, gradually pour in 1 cup of the hot milk. Transfer to saucepan. Add the remaining milk and cook over medium heat, whisking constantly, until it starts to coat the back of the spoon. Do not allow to boil. Remove from stove and whisk until cool. Strain with a very fine mesh. Store, covered with plastic wrap, in refrigerator until ready to use. Garnish with mint leaves before serving.

Serves 16

Poached Peaches with Blueberry Sauce
Barb Holland

Delicious, simple, and speedy with a microwave.

4	firm, ripe peaches	4
¼ cup	Cointreau, Amaretto, OR orange juice	50 mL
¼ cup	granulated sugar	50 mL
1 tbsp	cornstarch	15 mL
1 cup	blueberries OR raspberries	250 mL
1 tbsp	fresh lemon juice	15 mL

Halve peaches; remove pits. Place cut side up in a shallow 10- inch (25 cm) microwaveable dish. Pour liqueur or juice over peaches. Cover and microwave at High (100%) for 4 to 6 minutes or until peaches are tender. Cool peaches for 15 minutes. In a 4-cup (1 L) glass measuring cup or bowl, combine sugar and cornstarch. Pour liquid from peaches into cornstarch mixture and whisk until smooth. Stir in blueberries. Microwave, uncovered, at High for 2 to 4 minutes, or until mixture comes to a boil and thickens. Stir at least once partway through cooking. Stir in lemon juice. To serve, place two peach halves in each serving dish. Spoon sauce over peaches.

Makes 4 servings

Pears in Red Wine and Peppercorns
Marilyn Linton

This new twist on traditional poached pears offers fruit in a syrup with a bit of a bite. It's elegant on its own and wonderful, warm, with a bit of vanilla ice cream.

8	firm, ripe pears, peeled (stems left on)	8
	Juice of 1 lemon	
2 cups	dry red wine	500 mL
2 cups	water	500 mL
½ cup	honey	125 mL
12	whole cloves	12
3	cinnamon sticks	3
40	black peppercorns	40
1 piece	candied ginger	1

In a saucepan large enough to hold the pears, combine lemon juice, wine, water, honey, cloves, cinnamon, peppercorns, and candied ginger. Bring to a boil. Add pears and poach over medium heat for 10 to 15 minutes or until tender. Remove pears carefully with a slotted spoon. Strain syrup, then boil to thicken slightly. Spoon syrup over; serve warm or cold.

Makes 8 servings

Cointreau Quiver with Strawberries
Julia Aitken

Its name promises to bring giggles from guests but its taste will bring smiles. This rich, creamy confection sets slightly and quivers when brought to the table — hence its name.

1 ½ cups	sliced strawberries	375 mL
3 cups	milk	750 mL
⅓ cup	granulated sugar	75 mL
3 tbsp	water	50 mL
1 tbsp	unflavoured gelatin	15 mL
1 ⅔ cups	whipping cream	400 mL
3 tbsp	Cointreau	50 mL
8	whole strawberries	8
8	sprigs mint	8

Divide sliced strawberries among 8 large wine or dessert glasses; set aside. In large saucepan, combine 1 ½ cups (375 mL) milk and the sugar. Heat over medium heat for 3 to 5 minutes or until sugar dissolves; do not boil. Meanwhile, measure water into small bowl; sprinkle gelatin over water. Set aside to soften for 5 minutes. Then stand bowl in saucepan of hot water; stir 2 to 3 minutes or until gelatin is smooth and clear. Whisk gelatin mixture into hot milk, rinsing out bowl with a little of the hot milk and returning it to saucepan. Whisk in remaining milk, cream, and Cointreau. Divide mixture among the glasses. Chill, covered, in refrigerator overnight. Dessert will not set firm. Just before serving, cut a slit in each of the 8 whole strawberries. Slide one over edge of each glass. Garnish each dessert with sprig of mint.

Makes 8 servings

Ginger Fruit Bowl
Kate Bush

Fresh fruits at the end of a meal are often the perfect ending. This combination, with its spicy kick, is special.

1	cantaloupe, cut in chunks	1
1	fresh pineapple, cut in wedges	1
2	pink grapefruit, peeled, seeded, and sectioned	2
2	mangoes, peeled and cubed or thinly sliced	2
1 cup	fresh blueberries	250 mL
1- to 2-inch piece	fresh ginger	2.5 to 5 cm
2 tbsp	fresh lime juice	25 mL
2 tbsp	granulated sugar	25 mL
2 tbsp	light rum OR vodka	25 mL

Combine fruits in glass serving bowl. Peel and grate ginger. Squeeze to release juice. Add juice to fruit — approximately 1 tbsp (15 mL). Toss gently with remaining ingredients. Let stand for 30 minutes or more before serving.

Makes 4 servings

Irish Coffee
Mary McGrath

The perfect finish to a special dinner calls for Irish whiskey. No substitutes, says McGrath.

1 ½ oz	Irish whiskey	35 mL
1 to 2 tbsp	brown sugar	15 to 25 mL
	Strong black coffee	
	Whipped cream	

Into a warmed 8 oz (¼ L) stemmed heat-proof glass or coffee cup, pour the whiskey. Add sugar and fill to within ½ inch (1 cm) of top with very hot, strong black coffee. Stir to dissolve sugar. Fill to brim with chilled whipped cream. Try this as an alternative to coffee and liqueurs.

Makes 1 serving

Cranberry Orange Punch
Patricia Jamieson

*P*atricia Jamieson

learned to cook at Paris's

La Varenne Cooking

School. Over the years,

she has been a

restaurant co-owner and

pastry chef, a

food/product consultant

and a magazine test

kitchen home economist

and manager. She

joined Telemedia's

Eating Well *magazine as*

test kitchen director in

1990 where she tests 1500

recipes a year and

writes a column. She is

co-author of The Eating

Well Cookbook.

Use weak tea and perfect-looking fruit for a smashing punch that's so good (and rich in vitamin C) that it doesn't need booze.

1 quart	cranberry juice	1 L
2 cups	freshly brewed weak Orange Pekoe tea	500 mL
1	can (12½ oz/355 mL) frozen orange juice concentrate	1
1	ice ring (recipe follows), optional	1
1 quart	sparkling water OR soda water	1 L
12	orange OR tangerine slices	12
12	fresh mint sprigs	12

In a large container, combine cranberry juice, tea, and orange juice concentrate. Cover and refrigerate until chilled, or overnight. Just before serving, transfer to punch bowl. Gently add ice ring, if using, and pour in sparkling water or soda water. Garnish each glass with an orange or tangerine slice and a mint sprig.

Fruited Ice Ring:

2	tangerines OR oranges, thinly sliced	2
⅓ cup	cranberries	75 mL
10	sprigs fresh mint	10
6 cups (approx)	distilled water	1.5 L

Arrange about half of the tangerine or orange slices, cranberries, and mint sprigs decoratively on the bottom of a 6-cup (1.5 L) ring mold. Gently spoon in a little water to a depth of about ¼ inch (1 cm). Freeze until solid, about 1 hour. Pour in more water halfway up the sides of the mold. Freeze until solid, about 4 hours. Arrange the remaining tangerine or orange slices, cranberries, and mint sprigs over the ice. Gently pour in water until it fills the mold. Freeze until solid, at least 6 hours. Just before serving, dip the mold into hot water and invert the ice ring onto a plate. Gently slide into the punch bowl.

Makes 12 servings

Menus

Dinner Party with Fish
Creamy Squash Soup   Amontillado Sherry
Papillote of Fish with Carrots, Celery and Leeks   California Sauvignon Blanc
Wild Rice and Mushroom Pilaf
Steamed Green Beans
Mocha Pie

Buffet Dinner for 6 to 8
Tortilla Chips with Red Pepper Pesto
Chicken Pinwheels   Alsace Riesling
Seafood Casserole
Judith's Flank Steak   Côtes de Rhône; Village OR Red Zinfandel
Nutty Brown Rice
Whole Wheat Rolls
Ginger Fruit Bowl
Chocolate Almond Cake

Sunday Dinner
Peppery Pot Roast   Amarone
Green Salad
Bread and Butter Pudding

Barbecue
Bruschetta Pomodori on Backyard Grill
Sesame Soy Lamb Chops   Chilean Cabernet Sauvignon
Asparagus with Orange Vinaigrette
Apricot Peach Pie   Late harvest Riesling

Teenage Birthday Buffet
Penne with Italian Sausage, Tomato, and Herbs
Ribs Oriental Style
Carrots, Celery Sticks
Cranberry Orange Punch
Birthday Chocolate Layer Cake
Thumbprint Cookies

Summer Dinner Party
Gravlax with Dill   Muscadet-Sur-Lie
Tomato, Bocconcini, and Basil
Pasta with Shrimp, Zucchini, and Mushrooms   Sancerre
Peach Clafoutis

Light Dinner
Low-cal Caesar Salad with Shrimp
Seven Vegetable Broth with Walnut Garnish
Pork Tenderloin with Morels and Madeira   Mosel Riesling Kabinett
Steamed Asparagus
Poached Peaches with Blueberry Sauce

Spicy and Spirited
Cool Hand Cuke Cold Cucumber Soup
Hot Salt and Pepper Prawns
Spicy Thai Noodles   Alsace Muscat Niorico
Snow Pea with Mango Salad
Pears in Red Wine with Peppercorns
Sherbet or Ice Cream

Brunch
Sun-dried Tomato and Pesto Torta   Soave
Chinese Chicken Salad with Sesame and Ginger   Gewurtztraminer
Green Salad
Poached Peaches with Blueberry Sauce
Chocolate Mint Cookies

Taste of the Nations
Goat Cheese Salad with Arugula and Radicchio   Sancerre
Marinated Lamb   California Cabernet Sauvignon
Couscous with Chick Peas, Vegetables, and Raisins
Viennese Plum Cake   Asti Spumante

Vegetarian Dinner
Bistro-style Lentil Soup   Barbera
Ratatouille Casserole
Spinach with Nuts
Jamaican Rice and Peas
Golden Pear Pie

Little Meals for after the Game or Theatre
Smoked Salmon Pizza   Dry Sparkling Vouvray
Asparagus Wrapped in Prosciutto
Chocolate Pecan Pie

Baked Garlic with Warm Brie   California OR Australia Chardonnay
The Market Chowder
Steamed Ginger Apple Pudding

The Gourmet Club Cookoff
Smoked Trout Mousse   Pouilly Fumé
Pear and Celery Soup
Persian Roast Chicken with Apricot Sauce   Rheingau Riesling Spätlese
Sautéed Rappini and Fennel
French Potato Cake
Kathy's Lemon Supreme   Icewine

Index

A

Antipasto, 8
Appetizers
asparagus and prosciutto, 12
antipasto, 8
bruschetta, 7, 16
chicken breasts with broccoli, 4
endive with chèvre and shrimp,
11
garlic with Brie, 13
gravlax with dill, 5
nuts, 15
prawns, 70
red pepper pesto, 3
salmon
fillet of, 5
smoked, 2
spaghettini with asparagus, 121
spinach tofu dip, 10
sun-dried tomato and pesto torta,
9
Swiss cheese and garlic, 14
trout, smoked, 6
Apple
cake with caramel pecan sauce,
148
muffins, 162
pie, 170
steamed ginger pudding, 174
Apple cake with caramel pecan
sauce, 148
Apricot peach pie, 171
Apricot sauce, 54-55
Artichokes with fettucini, 108
Arugula, and goat cheese salad, 41
Asparagus
spaghettini with, 121
vinaigrette, 42
wrapped in prosciutto, 12
Asparagus with orange vinaigrette,
42
Asparagus wrapped in prosciutto,
12

B

Bacon and cauliflower soup, 28

Baked garlic with warm Brie, 13
Balsamic vinaigrette, 114
Barley, chicken cassoulet, 52
Basil
pesto sauce, 115
red pepper pesto, 3
Beef
chili with polenta, 82-83
cooked, salad, 77
filet, 78
flank steak, 79
pot roast, 80
Best apple pie muffins ever, The,
162
Birthday chocolate layer cake, 150
Biscuits, quick, 164
Bistro-style lentil soup, 33
Black bean cabbage, 94
Blueberries with poached peaches,
182
Bocconcini, and pasta, 114
Brandy snaps, 159
Brazil loaves, 141
Bread and butter pudding, 177
Broccoli, and chicken breast
appetizer, 4
Broth
Scotch, 27
vegetable, 24
Brown rice see Rice, brown
Bruschetta, 7, 16
Bruschetta pomodori, 7
Bulgur, tabbouleh, 46
Butter mocha icing, 150
Butterscotch sauce, 174

C

Cabbage with black beans, 94
Caesar salad with shrimp, 38
Cake
apple with caramel sauce, 148
Brazil loaves, 141
chocolate almond, 149
chocolate Bundt, 147
chocolate layer, 150
chocolate mousse, 144-45
chocolate roll, 143

hazelnut torte, 151
lemon, 142
matrimony, 153
strawberry rhubarb Linzer pie,
152
Viennese plum, 146
Caledonian cream, 186
Caramel pecan sauce, 148
Cauliflower and bacon soup, 28
Celery and pear soup, 22
Cheese
Brie with garlic, 13
bruschetta, 16
chèvre with endive and shrimp,
11
and garlic spread, 14
pasta shells stuffed with, 109
spaghetti squash with, 100
whole-wheat scones, 165
Chicken
breasts
with broccoli, 4
Chinese-style, 59
cranberry glazed, 53
Indian-style, 56
with lime, 58
salad, 60
tourtière, 88
Waldorf salad, 40
cooked, oriental noodle salad, 39
legs, peppercorn, 51
noodle salad, 39
pieces
baked Italian, 50
and barley cassoulet, 52
whole, Persian roast with apricot
sauce, 54-55
Chicken and barley cassoulet, 52
Chicken with lime, ginger, and
coriander, 58
Chicken pinwheels, 4
Chicken tikka, 56
Chili casserole with polenta, 82-83
Chilies, harissa sauce, 127
Chinese chicken salad with sesame
and ginger dressing, 60
Chinese-style
chicken breasts, 59

chicken salad, 60
Chocolate
 almond cake, 149
 Bundt cake, 147
 layer cake, 150
 lemon supreme, 180
 marquise, 181
 mint cookies, 161
 mousse cake, 144-45
 pecan pie, 169
 roll, 143
Chocolate almond cake, 149
Chocolate Bundt cake, 147
Chocolate marquise, 181
Chocolate mint cookies, 161
Chocolate pecan pie, 169
Chocolate roll, 143
Chowder
 clam, 32
 corn, 26
 fish, 30
Clam chowder supremo, 32
Clams, and pork chops, 90
Classic pesto sauce, 115
Cobbler, rhubarb, 176
Cod steaks Provençal, 69
Coffee, Irish, 188
Cointreau quiver with strawberries,
 184
Coleslaw, 43
Cookies
 brandy snaps, 159
 chocolate mint, 161
 double fudge, 158
 thumbprint, 160
Cool hand cuke cold cucumber
 soup, 20
Corn chowder, 26
Cornish game hens with
 lemongrass, 61
Cornmeal, polenta, 82
Couscous with chick peas,
 vegetables, and raisins, 126-27
Crabmeat
 chowder, 30
 creole, 68
Cranberry glazed chicken, 53
Cranberry orange punch, 187

Creamy squash soup, 25
Crystal fold, 59
Cucumber soup, 20
Curried lentils with coriander, 128

Date squares, 153
David's black bean cabbage, 94
Dessert *see also* Cake; Pie; Pudding
 Caledonian cream, 186
 chocolate marquise, 181
 cointreau with strawberries, 184
 fruit bowl, 185
 lemon supreme, 180
 pears in wine, 183
 poached peaches with blueberry
 sauce, 182
Dips, spinach tofu, 10
Double fudge cookies, 158
Double mushroom soup, 21
Dressing *see also* vinaigrette
 for chicken salad, 60
 cottage cheese, 38
 hazelnut, 45
 oriental-style, 39
 Waldorf salad, 40

Easiest-ever tomato soup, 23
Eggplant, ratatouille, 101
Endive with chèvre and shrimp, 11
Endives and ham "gratinés", 86

Fettucini with artichokes, 108
Fiesta bruschetta, 16
Fish *see also names of specific fish*
 papillote of, 64
 whole baked, 65
French potato cake, 95
French veal stew, 81
Fruit bowl, 185
Fruited ice ring, 187
Fudge cookies, 158

Garden stir fry, 102-103
Garlic with Brie appetizer, 13
Ginger fruit bowl, 185
Ginger, steamed apple pudding,
 174
Gingered turkey or pork scallopini,
 57
Goat cheese salad with arugula and
 radicchio, 41
Golden pear pie, 172
Gourmet tourtière, 88
Graham cracker, pie crust, 170
Gravlax with dill, 5

Haddock casserole, 67
Halibut, Provençal, 69
Ham, and endive, 86
Harissa sauce, 127
Hazelnut torte, 151
Hot salt and pepper prawns, 70

Ice ring, 187
Icing, butter mocha, 150
Indian-style
 chicken, 56
 curried lentils, 128
Irish coffee, 188
Italian baked chicken, 50

Jamaican rice and peas, 130
Jessie's biscuits, 164
Jiffy antipasto, 8
Judith's flank steak, 79

Kathy's lemon supreme, 180

Lamb
chops, sesame soy, 74
leg, marinated, 76
tenderloin, salad, 75
Lemon
cake, 142
herb rice, 135
supreme, 180
Lemon cake, 142
Lemon herb rice, 135
Lemongrass, and Cornish game
hens, 61
Lentil(s)
curried, 128
soup, 33
Lettuce salad with pistachios, 44
Linguine
with Brie cheese, 118
picante all'aglio e olivi, 117
with sausage, 110
Linguine with spicy sausage, 110
Linguini picante all'aglio e olivi,
117
Linzer pie, 152
Lobster
casserole, 67
potato salad, 36
stew, 31
Loin of veal with green apple
sauce, 84-85
Low-cal Caesar salad with shrimp,
38

_M_

Mango and snow pea salad, 45
Marinated lamb, 76
Market chowder, The, 30
Matrimony cake, 153
Meat _see_ Beef, Lamb, Pork, Veal
Michelle's killer linguini, 118
Michelle's lobster potato salad, 36
Mint chocolate cookies, 161
Mocha pie, 168
Mocha shortbread, 157
Mom's coleslaw, 43

Morels
and pork tenderloin, 87
spaghettini with asparagus and,
121
Mornay sauce, 86
Muffins
apple, 162
rhubarb, 163
Mushroom
linguini picante all'alglio e olivi,
117
soup, 21
and wild rice pilaf, 133
Mussels
lobster stew in, 31
steamed with tomatoes, 66

_N_

New Age Scotch broth, 27
Noodles, Thai-style, 122
North Thai spaghetti sauce, 120
Nuts, as appetizers, 15
Nutty brown rice, 129

_O_

Oatmeal shortbread, 156
Oriental chicken noodle salad, 39
Oriental-style
chicken noodle salad, 39
pork spareribs, 89
Oven roasted potatoes, 96

Papillote of fish with carrots,
celery, and leeks, 64
Pasta
cheese and tomato sauce, 109
fettucini with artichokes, 108
linguine with sausage, 110
linguini with Brie cheese, 118
linguini picante all'alglio e olivi,
117
penne with sausage and tomato,
111
ravioli, 119

with shrimp and zucchini, 112
spaghettini with asparagus and
morels, 121
Thai-style noodles, 122
Thai-style spaghetti sauce, 120
tomato and Bocconcini, 114
with tomatoes, basil and
Parmesan, 113
Pasta with fresh tomatoes, basil,
and Parmesan, 113
Pasta shells stuffed with cheese in a
creamy tomato sauce, 109
Pasta with shrimp, zucchini, and
mushrooms, 112
Peach clafoutis, 175
Peach(es)
apricot pie, 171
clafoutis, 175
poached with blueberry sauce,
182
Pear and celery soup, 22
Pear(s)
and celery soup, 22
pie, 172
in wine, 183
Pears in red wine and
peppercorns, 183
Peas _see_ snow pea; split pea
Pecan, chocolate pie, 169
P.E.I. lobster stew, 31
Penne with Italian sausage,
tomato, and herbs, 111
Pepper corn chicken, 51
Pepper, red, 3
Pepper steak, 78
Peppery pot roast, 80
Persian roast chicken and apricot
sauce, 54-55
Pesto
red pepper, 3
sauce, 115
sun-dried tomato, 116
Pie
apple, 170
apricot peach, 171
chocolate pecan, 169
mocha, 168
pear, 172

Pie crust, graham cracker, 170
Pierre's pepper steak, 78
Pilaf
  with pine nuts, 136
  wild rice and mushroom, 133
Pizza dough, 2
Plum cake, 146
Poached peaches with blueberry
    sauce, 182
Polenta, 82-83
Pork
  chops with clams, 90
  scallopini, 57
  spareribs, Oriental-style, 89
  tenderloin
    Chinese-style, 59
    with morels, 87
  Thai-style spaghetti sauce, 120
  tourtière, 88
Pork chops with clams, 90
Pork tenderloin with morels and
    Madeira, 87
Potato pie, 97
Potato(es)
  cake, 95
  and lobster salad, 36
  pie, 97
  roasted, 96
  salmon and fennel salad, 37
Prawns, hot salt and pepper, 70
Prosciutto, and asparagus, 12
Pudding
  bread and butter, 173
  peach clafoutis, 175
  steamed ginger apple, 174
Punch, cranberry orange, 187

Q

Quick pilaf with pine nuts, 136

R

Radicchio, and goat cheese salad,
    41
Rappini and fennel, sautéed, 98
Raspberries with poached peaches,
    182

Ratatouille casserole, 101
Ravioli with nutty cream sauce,
    119
Red and green leaf lettuce salad
    with pistachios and
    Parmesan, 44
Red pepper pesto, 3
Red snapper
  papillote of, 64
  whole baked, 65
Rhubarb
  cobbler, 176
  Linzer pie, 152
  muffins, 163
Rhubarb cobbler, 176
Ribs oriental style, 89
Rice
  brown, 129
    chicken with lime, 58
  lemon herb, 135
  and peas, 130
  pilaf with pine nuts, 136
  risotto with pine nuts and
    spinach, 131
  risotto with sausage and
    vegetables, 132
  with vegetables, 134
  with whole baked fish, 65
  wild
    chicken with lime, 58
    and mushroom pilaf, 133
Rice with fresh spring vegetables,
    134
Risotto
  with pine nuts and spinach, 131
  with sausage and vegetables, 132
Risotto with pine nuts and
    spinach, 131
Risotto with sweet sausage and
    vegetables, 132
Roasted fall vegetables, 105

S

Salad
  asparagus with orange
    vinaigrette, 42
  Caesar with shrimp, 38

chicken Chinese-style, 60
chicken noodle, 39
coleslaw, 43
goat cheese with arugula and
    radicchio, 41
lamb, 75
lettuce with pistachios, 44
lobster potato, 36
salmon, fennel and potato, 37
snow pea and mango, 45
Salmon
  chowder, 30
  fennel and potato salad, 37
  fillet of, 5
  papillote of, 64
  smoked, 2
Sauce
  apricot, 54-55
  butterscotch, 174
  caramel pecan, 148
  green apple, 84-85
  harissa, 127
  Mornay, 86
  pesto, 3, 115
Sausage
  with linguine, 110
  risotto with vegetables and, 132
Sautéed rappini and fennel, 98
Scallop
  casserole, 67
  chowder, 30
  creole, 68
Scones, whole-wheat seed, 165
Scotch broth, 27
Seafood casserole, 67
Seafood creole, 68
Sesame soy lamb chops, 74
Seven vegetable broth with walnut
    garnish, 24
Shortbread
  mocha, 157
  oatmeal, 156
Shrimp
  Caesar salad, 38
  chowder, 30
  creole, 68
  and endive appetizer, 11
  lobster stew in, 31

pasta with zucchini, 112
Smoked salmon pizza, 2
Smoked trout mousse, 6
Snaps, brandy, 159
Snow pea and mango salad with
    hazelnut dressing, 45
Soup *see also* Chowder
  cauliflower and bacon, 28
  cucumber, 20
  lentil, 33
  lobster, 31
  mushroom, 21
  pear and celery, 22
  Scotch broth, 27
  split pea, 29
  squash, 25
  tomato, 23
  vegetable, 24
Sour cream apple pie, 170
Spaghetti squash with a great deal
    of cheese, 100
Spaghettini with asparagus and
    morels, 121
Spicy nuts, 15
Spicy rhubarb muffins, 163
Spicy Thai noodles, 122
Spinach
  with nuts, 99
  risotto, 131
  tofu dip, 10
Spinach with nuts, 99
Spinach tofu dip, 10
Split pea soup, 29
Squares, date, 153
Squash
  soup, 25
  spaghetti with cheese, 100
Steamed ginger apple pudding, 174
Steamed mussels with tomatoes
    and fennel, 66
Stew
  chicken, 52
  lobster, 31
  veal, 81
Stir fry, vegetable, 102-103
Strawberry rhubarb Linzer pie, 152
Strawberry(ies)
  with cointreau, 184

rhubarb Linzer pie, 152
Stuffing for chicken, 54-55
Sun-dried tomato pesto, 116
Sun-dried tomato and pesto torta,
    9
Swiss cheese, garlic, and black
    pepper spread, 14
Swiss chocolate layered mousse
    cake, 144-45

T

Tabbouleh, 46
Terrific tabbouleh, 46
Terrine, vegetable, 104
Thai beef salad, 77
Thai-style
  beef salad, 77
  noodles, 122
  spaghetti sauce, 120
Three-layered vegetable terrine,
    104
Thumbprint cookies, 160
Tofu dip, 10
Tomato, Bocconcini, and basil in a
    balsamic vinaigrette, 114
Tomato(es)
  pasta with basil and Parmesan,
    113
  pasta with Bocconcini, 114
  soup, 23
  and steamed mussels, 66
  sun-dried and pesto, 9, 116
Torte, hazelnut, 151
Tortilla chips with red pepper
    pesto, 3
Tourtière, 88
Trout
  smoked, mousse, 6
  whole baked, 65
Turkey, scallopini, 57

V

Veal
  loin roast, 84-85
  stew, 81
Vegetable(s)

black bean cabbage, 94
broth, 24
potato(es), 95, 96, 97
rappini and fennel, 98
ratatouille, 101
with rice, 134
risotto with sausage and, 132
roasted fall, 105
spaghetti squash, 100
spinach, 99
stir fry, 102-103
terrine, 104
Viennese plum cake, 146
Vinaigrette, 37, 41
  balsamic, 114
  orange, 42

W

Waldorf salad, 40
Warm lamb salad Dijonnaise, 75
Warm salmon, fennel, and potato
    salad, 37
Whitefish
  fillets, papillote of, 64
  lobster stew, 31
  whole baked, 65
Whole baked fish with rice, 65
Whole-wheat seed scones, 165
Wild rice *see* Rice, wild
Wild rice and mushroom pilaf, 133
Wine and dessert, 140